It's Your First Year Teaching, but You Don't Have to Act Like It

Bob Kitchen

SCARECROWEDUCATION
Lanham, Maryland • Toronto • Oxford
2003

Published in the United States of America
by ScarecrowEducation
An imprint of The Rowman & Littlefield Publishing Group, Inc.
4501 Forbes Boulevard, Suite 200, Lanham, Maryland 20706
www.scarecroweducation.com

PO Box 317
Oxford
OX2 9RU, UK

British Library Cataloguing in Publication Information Available

Library of Congress Cataloging-in-Publication Data

Kitchen, Bob, 1956–
    It's your first year teaching, but you don't have to act like it / Bob
Kitchen.
        p.   cm.
    ISBN 1-57886-029-6 (pbk. : alk. paper)
    1. First year teachers–United States–Handbooks, manuals, etc.
2. Teacher effectiveness–United States–Handbooks, manuals, etc.
I. Title.
LB2844.1.N4 K55 2003
371.1—dc22   2003015228

∞ ™ The paper used in this publication meets the minimum
requirements of American National Standard for Information
Sciences—Permanence of Paper for Printed Library Materials,
ANSI/NISO Z39.48-1992. Manufactured in the United States of
America.

CONTENTS

PREFACE

My name is Bob Kitchen, and I've dedicated twenty-one years of my professional life to teaching. I began in a rural environment, subbed on a long-term basis in an urban setting, and I just recently completed my sixteenth year at my current school, located in the suburbs. This is where I plan to finish my career. But I've been one of the lucky ones . . . I survived.

When I was growing up, my mom was a substitute teacher (she subbed for twenty-five years), and most of my academic success throughout elementary and junior high school I attribute to her. Each night she assisted my brother, sister, and me with our homework and quizzed us using index cards as we prepared for tests. She was our "teacher," and from her we learned the values of patience and paying attention to detail. Throughout my high school years and then into college, it wasn't about what profession I would pursue, it was only which subject I would choose to teach. Coupled with my love of writing was a desire to coach, so I knew that education was "right" for me. Then, after a wonderful student teaching experience, I eagerly awaited my first job as a professional educator.

However, something went drastically wrong. After only three short years on the job, I not only despised the profession, I desperately sought a way to escape it. Unfortunately, my situation was not an isolated one. In fact, this year, colleges nationwide will issue nearly 200,000 education degrees, yet only half of those will ever see the inside of their first classroom. But what's most disturbing is that a growing percentage of those who begin a teaching career will abandon the profession within their first three to five years. Thus, as a nation, we are on the brink of a devastating teacher shortage, and unless we discover a solution, our children are the ones who will suffer.

Why are we losing good teachers? Is it money? I certainly understand that some leave because they can obviously earn a better income in a different occupation. Do some prospective educators change their minds or career goals? Without question. But what about the rest? Why are literally thousands of quality teachers fleeing our profession? I'm writing this book to provide at least a small part of the solution, and most importantly, to keep good teachers—*like you*—teaching.

At this very moment, college professors in senior-level methods classes are instructing students how to formulate detailed lesson plans that include specific goals and performance-based objectives. They're also discussing the significance of implementing a wide variety of teaching strategies to meet the various needs of today's students. They're undoubtedly covering visual, auditory, and kinesthetic learning styles as well as inclusion, learning disabilities, 504 plans, and IEPs. In fact, most colleges do an outstanding job of preparing future educators in nearly all areas. However, unless college students have an instructor who is also a high school teacher or someone who has recently been in a high school classroom, it is extremely difficult to teach *practical* classroom management and discipline strategies for today's teens. Unfortunately, these two areas are likely responsible for driving more individuals out of our profession than all of the others combined.

Despite the passion you might feel toward your subject and the overwhelming knowledge you possess, it's all wasted if you can't manage and control your students. For some, this is a seemingly innate talent, a gift. However, for the rest of you, either you'll learn on the job (like I did) and if you survive the first few years "on your own" you'll improve with experience, or you'll read my book to help supplement what you learned (or didn't learn) in college.

I'm going to provide you with some practical ideas that you can use *immediately*. I will begin by teaching you the importance of finding a job both in a building and a district that is "right" for you. Then, I'll discuss at length how to begin the process of meticulous preparation for your first position. Next, I'll cover the specifics of knowing what to say as well as how and when to say it on your very first day. Finally, and perhaps most importantly, I'll provide you with various tips and strategies that you can implement regarding classroom management and discipline issues that will help make your first year the successful start of a long, rewarding tenure as a professional educator.

Is it possible to prepare you for every problem you may encounter in your classroom? Of course not. But after reading my book, you'll feel more confident that you can intelligently and professionally handle just about anything that comes your way. Dealing with everyday discipline problems and managing your classroom effectively will allow you to do what you spent the last four years of your life preparing to do—teach.

INTRODUCTION

June 2003 marked the end of my twenty-first year of teaching. It's almost unfathomable that when my daughter, who entered second grade last fall, reaches her junior year of high school, I will be retiring (at age fifty-five). However, even after 21 years, as the upcoming summer approaches, I'm already looking forward to next school year. I've spent more than two decades of my professional life in a high school classroom, yet I'm still excited about teaching kids!

You've chosen a wonderful profession. We need people just like you—young, energetic, enthusiastic, filled with new and innovative ideas. The feeling I get when I talk with kids, laugh with kids—*when I teach kids*—is unlike any other. But it wasn't always this way for me. I made some egregious errors in my very first teaching assignment that led to teacher burnout, three career changes, and serious self-doubts, before finally returning to the classroom . . . where I belonged.

Many of the mistakes that I made in the beginning could have been prevented. In fact, shortly after I started my first full-time teaching job, I realized just how unprepared I was. Despite my thorough knowledge of the subject matter, I was simply not ready to take command of thirty students. That first teaching assignment almost drove me permanently away from education, and that's precisely the reason why I'm writing this book. I can assist you in your transition from college and student teaching to not only securing your first full-time teaching position, but to surviving your first year in the classroom. As confident (or terrified) as you feel right now, first read this book. I love my job, and I want you to feel the same way as I do after your twenty-first year in the profession.

ONE

Finding the "Right" School

YOUR FIRST DECISION IS YOUR
MOST IMPORTANT ONE

You made it! You finished your classes, completed your student teaching, and received your degree. It's now time to start seriously searching for that first full-time position, right? Not yet! Before you begin, heed this very important piece of advice: Do not accept a teaching job unless it is "right" for you.

Let me explain. Although many graduates eagerly accept that first job offer—as I did—this is potentially a huge mistake. In fact, accepting the wrong position could ruin any chance you have for a lengthy career in education. I realize that after four years of college, which also included your sixteen-week student teaching experience, you undoubtedly feel that you are ready for your own classroom, your own students, and your own paycheck. You desperately long to afford the basic necessities in life. I vividly remember how you feel. However, it's crucial that you be patient in your job search. Despite what you might have heard, don't be hoodwinked into believing that all schools are alike and that no matter where you teach, "Kids are kids." I made that mistake, and I want you to learn from it.

My first job offer was from a school I'd never even heard of. Even though it was only thirty-five miles east of where I'd been born and raised, I didn't have the faintest idea where the school was located. I certainly wasn't ready to teach there. Growing up in a middle-class suburban high school and attending a conservative Midwestern college, I

1

wasn't prepared to teach in a rural district, a culture I knew nothing about. *Cut tobacco? Bail hay? Smell manure?* Not in my world! Do you think any of my college professors (or anyone else for that matter) prepared me for dealing with students who missed school because they had to help out on the family farm? Did they warn me that only 8 percent of the graduating seniors in my first year of teaching would attend college? Can you imagine how shocked I was (as a serious educator) when I learned that we would get three school holidays in late September for the county fair? No, I wasn't ready for this!

Could the transition have been smoother and I more comfortable in this school if I had first taught somewhere else and gained some experience in an *environment similar to the one in which I was raised?* Without question. In a rural high school environment, I soon discovered that I not only didn't understand their world, I didn't belong in it. Because my brother, sister, and I had all attended college, I naively thought most—if not all—kids would have the desire to pursue some level of postsecondary education. But during my first three years of teaching, an average of less than 20 percent of the graduating seniors attended college! I also thought that most—if not all—parents would attend open house and parent–teacher conferences. My mom and dad always did. However, I once sat for eight consecutive hours in my classroom and only met with two sets of parents (out of my 140 total students).

The members of my first school community included some of the kindest individuals I've ever come across in my twenty-year career, but in many ways I was an alien to their world. I wasn't raised in a rural environment, and I knew nothing of their way of life. In hindsight, maybe I could have been more flexible and done a better job of adapting, but I didn't know how. I wasn't ready. No one ever warned me that anything like this could happen!

Discouraged, frustrated, and angry after only three years of what I hoped would be my "lifelong profession," I quit education altogether. And I wouldn't have returned if a close friend hadn't convinced me to give it one more try, but this time in a school district more similar to the type that I had attended. I am forever grateful to him.

Don't repeat my mistake! Even if you are one of those rare individuals who can easily adapt to a variety of situations, do *not* accept your first job in a district that is totally foreign to the one that you attended. A tremendous amount of stress and pressure automatically accompany your first year of teaching, so don't exacerbate the situation by having to adjust to a totally different student and parent mind-set than what you are accustomed to.

SUMMARY

Be patient in your job search! Wait for a position to open up in a district similar to the one where you attended or at the very least where you completed your student teaching. Attend job fairs, remain in touch with your college's placement office, and send out your applications to schools that would be a good fit for you. Allow one to two weeks for a response; then, if you don't hear back, pick up the phone and call. You must be aggressive and sell yourself. Don't wait for them to make the first move. When you call—and always call the superintendent's office—first ask if your application was received, and second, if there are any openings. If the answer is "No" to your second query, end with a very polite, "Thank you for you time, but if something does open up, I'd really appreciate it if you could keep me in mind for an interview." Remember that several jobs will open up in mid- to late July, but there are also many teachers hired well into August because of illness, pregnancy, and job transfers. On occasion, sometimes at the last minute, teachers unexpectedly leave one district to go to another. Be patient!

If you don't find the "right" job and the school year begins, sign up to be a substitute teacher in the district or districts of your choice. Nearly every school district is in desperate need of subs, and as far as you're career is concerned, it's a tremendous opportunity to learn the profession firsthand (without all the responsibilities of a full-time teacher) and get paid for doing so. Subbing brings about a totally separate teaching philosophy—especially when you might be in a particular classroom for only one or two days at a time. And sometimes long-term sub assignments turn into full-time teaching positions! Finally, in some states (you need to check with your superintendent or your state Department of Education), if you substitute teach for a major percentage of a school year, you might receive credit for a full year of teaching.

Let's proceed with the best-case scenario at this juncture. You've accepted a job in a district that is indeed "right" for you. Now that you've officially been hired, the next stage, the planning stage, is crucial.

Two

Preparation . . . The Days, Weeks, and (Sometimes) Months Before

COLLECT, ORGANIZE, AND PREPARE!

Your date of hire will dictate how long you have to prepare for your initial day of class. But as soon as you accept that first job, remember that the more organized you remain, the better chance you have of succeeding, especially your first year.

No matter how rewarding or enjoyable your student teaching assignment was and how comfortable you were, your first full-time position will be a totally different experience. Despite how much you think you know right now, nothing compares to the feeling you'll have when the final bell sounds and you close your door on that very first day. Although friends, administrators, and colleagues might try to assuage any of your fears by telling you, "Don't worry; you'll be fine," don't be naïve. When you close your classroom door, it's only you, and if you aren't prepared, you will fail.

I'm not denying that you've dealt with pressure already, and at no time during this book is my tone meant to be condescending, but now, you're a professional—at least you're supposed to be. Very few occupations require you to be as prepared and organized on a daily basis as teaching, so you must spend the majority of your time up until that first day getting yourself ready.

GET ORGANIZED

As soon as you're hired, the first thing you should do is buy four legal pads of paper because, as you begin to gather facts and develop questions and concerns, you must write everything down! You undoubtedly gathered a plethora of information during the interview process at your new school, including a student handbook, teacher handbook, code of conduct, curriculum guide, etc., so take your four legal pads and categorize them as follows:

Legal Pad #1: Questions and Concerns

As you read through your student and faculty handbooks and code of conduct, focus on the various rules, regulations, and policies that govern your school and record any questions or concerns that you might have. It is essential that you understand all matters related to discipline to avoid a potential "situation," which is anything that requires more than a simple admonishment to a student.

For example, is it okay to discipline a student by sending him to the office? How about out in the hall? Does your school give detentions, and if so, what paperwork (if any) is involved? What rule violations warrant detentions and which warrant suspensions? Are suspended students allowed to make up the work they miss? Is there a school rule governing the amount of time a student gets to complete make-up work after an excused absence?

Perhaps these questions will have already been answered after you've read through all your materials, but if not, first ask your department head or your mentor (a veteran teacher assigned to assist a "rookie" during that first year). Then, if you still have concerns, ask your assistant principal, who by job description at most schools, is in charge of discipline. You obviously can't anticipate everything that could possibly occur, and many times a potential situation can be avoided with a little common sense. However, before your first day in the classroom, gather as much information as possible, read and study it thoroughly, and then ask as many questions as you deem necessary.

For example, where does your class go during fire and tornado drills? How about getting supplies, like a tape dispenser or a stapler? Does your school provide them? And, if you are assigned a duty (i.e., study hall, cafeteria duty), what rules apply? Write down every question that you have, and perhaps even more importantly, once you learn the answer from your principal, your assistant principal, your mentor, or your department chairperson, again, write it down!

Legal Pad #2: Points of Emphasis

Have this pad of paper with you or close by at all times! During the conversations you'll have with administrators and fellow colleagues before your first day, you'll often hear expressions like, "You don't want to forget this," "This is really important," "If you don't remember anything else, don't forget this," or "This is something you might want to consider." Write everything down on this pad! Then, review the information repeatedly as you get closer to your first day.

Legal Pad #3: Things to Do

Pages might be torn from this pad on a weekly or even daily basis. Include all tasks you must complete and purchases you must make to prepare yourself for the school year. The following are a few entries that should appear on everyone's "Things to Do" legal pad before the first day of school:

1. Contact the head of your department. If you didn't have the opportunity to meet or talk with your department chairperson at length during the interview process, do this first. Be sure you know what classes you'll be teaching and obtain a curriculum guide (also referred to as "course of study") as well as a copy of a teacher's textbook for each of your classes. Remember that the rookies often get stuck with the classes no one else wants, but that's pretty standard procedure at most schools. Just collect all of your materials as soon as you can so that you can begin mapping out your plan (syllabus) for the first quarter.
2. Learn as much as you can about your students and the town. You can gain this knowledge by asking the principal for a staff phone directory and then calling at least two teachers who are veterans

on the faculty and two more who are newer to the district. (The principal will provide you with this information. Or, if you don't feel comfortable asking the principal, ask the secretary in the main office or at the board of education office.) Ask fellow faculty members about district and parent expectations as well as any tips they might consider helpful. I'll never forget one piece of advice that I received from a veteran teacher: "Don't ever do anybody any favors, and it won't come back to screw you in the end." Translation: If the grading scale dictates that a student must earn a 93 percent or higher to earn an A, don't ever round up. If you do decide to round up, even if that student has a 92.9 average, you'd better do this for everyone. If you aren't consistent, you can count on phone calls from parents as well as from your building principal.

Finally, don't worry about "bothering" any of the experienced teachers you decide to call. They will be thrilled (in most cases, even honored) that you are soliciting their opinion.

3. Visit your new school as often as possible. Become familiar with the exact route as well as alternate ones (in case of traffic or road construction). Don't take a chance on ever being late that first year. Try to arrive at least ten minutes before you are required to be at school each day of your first year of teaching. Being habitually tardy could make your stay at that school a short one.

During your numerous visits to school, you'll probably see both the principal and assistant principal on more than one occasion. You want to be recognized as someone who is willing to put in the time to be organized and prepared. Your administrators are obviously important people to have in your corner, so try to get to know them a little. (I didn't say "suck up"—just be friendly and willing to learn). Always appear eager to accept whatever advice they can give you to help make your transition smoother, and be sure you write down whatever they offer. Be sure to ask the assistant principal any discipline-related questions you might have after studying the student handbook or code of conduct.

4. Introduce yourself to all support staff, including secretaries, maintenance workers, and cafeteria employees and let them

know that you're looking forward to working with them. Perhaps you became acquainted with these individuals during the interview process, but if not, ask if they have any advice for the "new kid" as well as if there is anything you can do to make their job easier. You will make an immediate impression! More importantly, you are letting them know that you will be working *with* them and that you will treat them as equals, not subordinates. Don't ever forget that there are very few lifelines more important to you at your new school than the secretarial and maintenance staff.

From distributing the basic essentials, such as chalk, tape, staplers, pens, and pencils, to helping you send a fax or run the copying machine, the secretaries will be invaluable assets, especially during your first year. The custodians not only have keys for every door and lock in the school, they know how everything works so they can either fix what's broken or get you what you need, such as extra file cabinets, shelves, desks, etc. Few people know more about the inner workings of the district than the secretaries and maintenance staff. If you always treat these individuals with respect and remember to say "Please" and "Thank you," you'll be amazed at how much they can help make your first year (and all future years) run more smoothly.

5. Introduce yourself to the school treasurer, the guidance counselor(s), and the special education teacher(s). Simply say, "My name is (your name), and I just wanted to stop by and say hello." Then, before you leave, be sure to end with "It was really nice meeting you." Do not underestimate the significance the treasurer plays in your teaching career. If you ever need your paycheck a day early, some assistance with paperwork regarding tuition reimbursement (some districts pay for graduate classes toward your master's degree), advice on certification or licensure, or help establishing a tax-sheltered annuity, the treasurer is the person you'll normally contact. Again, just by introducing yourself and being courteous enough to end with "It was nice meeting you" could greatly pay off during your first year.

   Next, introduce yourself to the guidance counselor(s), who are just as crucial to your first year running smoothly as the support staff. First, ask if he or she could please provide you with a copy of your class lists as well as any background information on any students with special needs or unusual circumstances. For example, our counselors will often leave us a voice mail if a student's parent is undergoing a major operation or suffering from a serious illness. This lets me know to be more flexible with that student concerning assignments and tests.

Finally, you need to meet the special education teachers, who are vital cogs in the success of all schools nowadays. As a classroom teacher, you will work closely with these individuals whose job it is to assist the growing number of special-needs children with learning disabilities. In fact, you might even have a special education teacher in your class; I am fortunate enough to team-teach one period each day with a special educator, and it's been a tremendous learning experience. She has helped me understand the specific needs of various students who suffer from myriad learning disabilities and to recognize the most effective way to help them be successful in the classroom.

6. If you are fortunate enough to have your own room, make it a place you will be proud of and excited about every day. First, don't panic if you don't get your own classroom. Many rookie teachers are stuck traveling from room to room, keeping their materials on a cart. It's difficult, but if you want to be a part of a quality district, you might have to contend with this type of inconvenience your first few years. However, if you do get your own classroom, decorate and make it as colorful and lively as possible. My school's colors are blue and gold, and I took a few days out of the summer before I started teaching at my new school to decorate. First, using an opaque projector, I traced in pencil "Madeira Pride" about eight-inches tall on one wall, "The time is now . . . go for it!" on another wall, and "Confidence" on the third (my fourth wall is all windows). I then painted in the letters with bright royal blue and gold paint, which the school paid for.

I also started a tradition that first year of collecting photographs of each of my ninth-grade students when they were two, three, or four years old, and these are currently on display in my room. I post them by the door, and the students enjoy guessing the identity of each of their classmates. I've labeled this collection of photographs after the popular soap opera, calling them, *All My Children*. In addition to teaching English to my students, I also coach cross country. The maintenance men have been kind enough to put up shelves at the top of every wall, where I display seventy-seven championship trophies as well as dozens of pictures of past runners. Finally, if there is glass anywhere near the door allowing your students to see what's going on in the hallway (or allowing those outside to view what's going on in your room), seal it off with dark construction paper or pictures. This will help to eliminate distractions, which obviously prevent you from doing your job.

Be as creative as possible, but give your room an identity, a personality—*your personality*. As trite as it sounds, every morning I am extremely proud of what I see. Parents, students, and visitors love to see my room. Not only does it reflect the pride that I feel in being a teacher and coach, but when students see the trophies, the slogans, and the infusion of blue and gold adorning all four walls, it sends the message that my enthusiasm, energy, and expectations are high.

7. Organize your room. Once the decorating is completed, now it's time to arrange your desks the way you want them. For example, do you want your students seated in rows, or are you a fan of the semicircle? How about one big circle? One of our teachers has a large pathway in the middle of the room with her desks arranged symmetrically in rows on opposite sides. Try arranging them in a variety of ways as you stand in front and look out at your classroom. However, if you're uncertain at this time, I'd recommend the traditional rows. You can always reorganize once you have established control and feel more comfortable after the first few weeks (or months) of school. It's one of the many decisions that you get to make early on, but unless you feel strongly about it, stay in rows.

Once the desks are arranged, be certain that you check your

class lists to see that you have enough desks. If not, talk to the maintenance staff or your principal to get what you need, and if possible one or two extras, just in case of new students or last-minute schedule changes.

Next, find a spot in your room where you will stand and address your students when it is time to begin class. This has been a very valuable strategy for me that I learned many years ago from a veteran teacher. After all, you don't want to shout at the beginning of each class, "Okay, let's get quiet! That was the bell! Sit down and be quiet, please!" This is a complete waste of your time and energy, yet many teachers—including some veterans who should know better—feel compelled to yell at the start of every class to gain their students' attention. In my room, students know that when I stand behind my lectern, they'd better be totally silent or the work we plan to do that day in class becomes homework. It's amazing how quickly they catch on!

Organize your textbooks (if you have them) and be sure you have enough for everyone. Then find a spot that's out of your way and stack them neatly until you distribute them. (I'll address later when the best time is to pass out books.) If you don't have enough, you'll simply have to make copies of anything you plan to use from the text.

Finally, be sure you have adequate storage space for your personal items. Hopefully, you'll be given at the very least a file cabinet (that locks) for your papers and personals. If not, ask for one, and always be on the lookout for extra shelves or cabinets that other teachers are discarding. You can never have enough room for all of your "stuff." Again, by befriending the maintenance staff early on, they might be able to help you in this area.

8. Organize your desk. Now that your classroom is decorated and desks and textbooks are organized, it's time to focus on your desk. Don't be alarmed if that first year you not only don't have your own room, you don't even have your own desk. Deal with it! As I previously mentioned, if this is a quality district that you want to be part of for years to come, you might encounter several inconveniences your first year—get used to it. However, if you do have

your own desk, I prefer not to instruct you how to organize it, for it's a strictly a matter of personal preference. I will instead let you know the materials you must have in or on that desk to be organized and thereby successful. The basic necessities—pens, pencils, and chalk—are fairly obvious, but here is my list for the Top 20 of everything else you definitely need (and these appear in no certain order):

- Computer: Many schools will provide you with one, but if not, this is a necessity. At our school, we keep all of our grades on computer, making grade books nearly obsolete. I have nearly twenty years of tests, handouts, notes, and so on stored on files in my computer that ensure organization and preparation.
- Desktop calendar: This is a tremendous way to write down upcoming meetings, appointments, and similar events. If you don't write it down, you run the risk of forgetting it, and first-year teachers cannot afford to miss faculty meetings, 504 or IEP meetings for "special needs" students (more about these later), parent–teacher conferences, etc.
- Post-It Notes and index cards: The more Post-It Notes you have the better, and always buy the colorful ones. I use my desktop calendar, the side of my file cabinet, and often part of my blackboard to post reminders. Next, buy at least 200 3"- × - 5" index cards that you will use for textbook information.
- Stapler and staples: You'll be surprised how often you (and your students) use a stapler.
- Clear tape and dispenser: It sounds trivial, but trying to figure out where the new piece of clear tape begins on a roll requires fingernails and patience, and it's a hassle you can easily avoid by having a dispenser. If your school does not provide one, buy your own.
- Roll of masking tape: Pictures won't adhere for any length of time to concrete walls with clear tape—you must use masking tape.
- Dictionary: Always have one handy for obvious reasons. Writing words on the board without knowing the correct spelling is only going to make one person look stupid (that would be you).

- Ruler: This might be needed only two or three times a year (unless you're a math teacher), but get one anyway.
- Calculator: You'll use one for a variety of reasons.
- Gum, mints, or Listerine oral care strips: There's not much worse than being around people with halitosis. Do you remember a particular teacher from high school whose breath was so bad that you had to hold yours when conversing to avoid passing out? Just chew gum or continually have a breath mint handy. Your students will greatly appreciate it!
- A small mirror: This is crucial! Especially on that first day, but also every morning thereafter, you should check to see that you have nothing in the corner of your eyes or hanging around inside of your nose. Your hair should be neatly in place, clothes neatly pressed. Guys, make sure your tie is straight! Girls should go easy on the perfume and the make-up, and guys should stay away from the cologne. Students will form an impression of you immediately, and you certainly want that first one to be positive. You might not always be able to get to the teacher's lounge or bathroom to check your appearance one last time before class, so have a small mirror in your room (you can keep it in your desk).
- Comb or brush: This one's fairly obvious. The windblown look is not "in"—neither is "bedhead."
- Six boxes of tissues: You'll be surprised how many students will either ask you for a tissue or sit in class and sniff incessantly, distracting you and everyone else. Six boxes should last you the entire year.
- Liquid soap: This is a really important one. Always wash your hands before lunch and immediately after grading papers, for until you settle into a routine and build up immunity, first-year teachers are much more susceptible to illness than the veterans. I contracted mononucleosis two weeks into my very first year of teaching and missed eight days of school. Since then, I've never missed (because of illness) more than five days during an entire school year.
- Plenty of extra pencils and paper: Not just for you, but you also have to anticipate a percentage of your students being forget-

ful, unorganized, or apathetic. You certainly don't want constant distractions by allowing kids to run to their lockers for writing utensils or paper.

- Functional pencil sharpener: Most rooms will have one, but often times they are broken or don't function properly. When in doubt, ask for a new one or simply buy your own. (But don't get an electric one—it's a distraction!)
- Paper clips: You'll use these all the time to keep papers, memos, and similar items together.
- A clock that works: You should already have one in your room, but if not, purchase one and put it on your desk. (I'd also recommend wearing a wristwatch.)
- Some type of snack: Always have something to eat in your desk. I keep cheese and peanut-butter crackers (the ones in the store that are already packaged) as well as some caramels or Hershey kisses. I almost always indulge in some type of midmorning snack between classes.
- Some type of anti-diarrhea medicine: Imagine having to deliver one of the most important speeches of your life—which is what you'll be doing on your first day—faced with the possibility of having to leave the room at any given moment in a dead sprint.

Feel free to add some if you wish, but you'll always be prepared if you at least stick to these twenty.

9. Compose a letter of introduction that you will send home with each student. This is a tremendous opportunity for you as a new teacher to immediately develop a positive relationship with parents. (See sample letter.)
10. Look over your class lists, and then ask at least two veteran teachers (as well as the guidance counselors) if they would mind checking them over to let you know of potential troublemakers. Next, make up your seating charts with these students right in front of you. Don't be surprised if you find some of the kids labeled by others as "trouble" are just the opposite. However, either way, you win. Whether they are potential discipline prob-

Figure 2.1   Sample Introduction Letter

Tuesday, August 22

Dear Parent(s):

My name is Bob Kitchen, and I am thrilled to have the opportunity to teach your child this year. I'm originally from right here in the city, having graduated from White Springs High School and then from Alexander University. My mom was a teacher in the White Springs school system for 25 years, and my brother and brother-in-law are also teachers.

Writing has always been a passion of mine, and I'm eagerly awaiting the challenge of helping your child improve his reading and writing skills in my class. Should you ever have any questions, please feel free to call me at school (Voicemail #546).

This year's "Back to School Night" is on Wednesday, September 18. If I don't hear from you before then, I'll look forward to seeing you there.

Sincerely,

Bob Kitchen

lems or they end up being some of your favorites, you already have them right up front.

11. Type up a general syllabus for the first quarter as well as a sheet that details your grading information. Then, run off enough copies for each student and stack these neatly on top of your desk. Don't list too many specifics, just a very general overview of what you plan to accomplish based on your curriculum guide. Remember that there is no way you can accurately place a timetable on learning, especially when dealing with teenagers, so these plans could change (sometimes on a daily basis). (See sample syllabus and grading information sheet.)

Whatever you decide to give to your students, make enough copies for everyone well in advance of your first day; if you wait until the last minute, you might not have time to get them done! (Hopefully, your school will have a copy machine that will be at your disposal. If not, go to an office supply store or printer and pay to have them made.)

Figure 2.2   Sample Syllabus

Syllabus for Honors English 9

Quarter #1

Vocabulary . . . 25 new words every week, quizzes every Wednesday and Friday

Grammar . . . Emphasis on parts of speech, identifying word functions in sentences, and rules of commas

Writing . . . 2–3 one-page typed assignments, topics to be announced

Literature . . . *Merchant of Venice* (read entirely during class)

Speech . . . Each student will deliver two speeches, topics to be announced

---

Legal Pad #4: Ideas

Any thoughts or ideas you have on the art of teaching or how you want to present what you discover and collect through research should be recorded on this pad. Your department head and some of your fellow teachers will hopefully offer assistance regarding subject matter, including sharing ideas that did or did not work or providing you with recommendations on meeting the needs of specific students. If they don't offer, ask! There is also a tremendous amount of information you can obtain via the Internet; write it all down and keep it organized.

Finally, purchase a small tape recorder and keep it in your car. Whenever you are driving, be sure you have your recorder with you. Turn off the radio and allow yourself to think; any ideas that pop into your head, simply press "record" and begin talking. If you're sitting in the doctor's or dentist's office or find yourself waiting for an oil change, have your

Figure 2.3   Sample Grading Information Sheet

Grading	
The grading scale is as follows:	
93–100	A
85–92	B
77–84	C
70–76	D
Below 70	F

---

tape recorder or one of your legal pads with you. Also, try to keep one of these close to your bed at night. I realize that this might sound peculiar to some, but many of the best and most creative ideas you have might come to you at the most inopportune times, such as while you are driving or while you are in bed getting ready to go to sleep. If you're like me, you don't want to get out of your bed once you're in it. Be prepared, and always write everything down (or record it)!

THREE

A Support System Is Crucial

If at all possible, live at home during your first year of teaching. As a new educator, you'll need a strong support system to assist you through your first teaching job, and your family can be invaluable for this. Having someone close by who will listen to you, perhaps offering some practical advice or occasionally providing a little pep talk, can help overcome some of the many hurdles you encounter that first year. Teaching can be an extremely lonely profession at times, and having your parents or even your siblings nearby can be a tremendous benefit.

Another advantage to staying at home is that you'll be able to get your finances in order. I'm not suggesting you freeload—you should at least pay a small fee for room and board—but it won't be as expensive as renting an apartment. You will then be able to save a significant amount of cash, which will enable you to possibly pay off student loans, get a reliable car, and start on your tax-sheltered annuity program. This is yet another serious mistake that I made! You should immediately invest at least 10 percent of every paycheck into a 403b plan, which I cover in chapter 23.

If living with family is not possible, sharing an apartment or a house with another teacher is your second-best option. Again, a support system is crucial, and although a nonteacher roommate is better than living alone that first year, most noneducators just don't understand what it's like to be a teacher.

Finally, if you do end up renting an apartment or house, the optimal situation would be to live out of the district but no farther than thirty minutes away from your new school. Do not live in your new district, at least the first year. If you live too close to school, it's too tempting for unexpected visitors (students), and you should never allow students into your house or apartment! It only takes one immature or misguided teenager to allege sexual misconduct and ruin any hopes you had of a teaching career. Nowadays, in alleged cases of sexual misconduct or impropriety, you'll have little defense if you allowed that student into your home. Even if the visit was totally harmless and you're proven innocent, your reputation will be tarnished and any hopes of a long-term career (at least in that district) will be greatly diminished.

During my first year, I normally went out with friends on Friday nights, but on one particular occasion, I was home alone in my apartment. Even though it was late, when I heard the knock, I simply thought some friends had dropped by, so without even glancing through the peephole I opened the door . . . only to discover two of my female students. No one warned me in college that this situation could ever occur, but fortunately I had the common sense not to allow them inside my apartment.

The following Monday I informed my principal what had occurred, and he told me I had acted judiciously. He also recommended that I talk to these girls and let them know in a stern manner that it was inappropriate for them to visit me at home. I heeded his advice, and no student ever again dropped by.

FOUR

Without This, You'll Never Make It

Maintaining a sense of humor is unequivocally the most important character trait necessary to surviving in the teaching profession for any length of time. If you can't laugh with your students—as well as at yourself—you are destined for misery and failure.

During my first year of teaching, one of the many mistakes I made was that I began the year taking myself way too seriously, and I attribute this to being totally overwhelmed. I was teaching six classes (three different preparations), coaching every day after school, and in addition, I had been assigned to the duty most veteran teachers avoid—cafeteria duty. I really didn't learn to laugh and recognize the importance of maintaining my sense of humor until shortly before Thanksgiving, when the following incident occurred while on cafeteria duty.

At the very end of the lunch period on that day, I was making one final stroll around the cafeteria, picking up bits of paper and discarding a few stray milk cartons. Suddenly, without warning, I observed something no first-year teacher ever wants to see. Written neatly in ketchup (from the squirt bottles provided by the cafeteria), directly in the middle of a table, were the words "Mr. Kitchen Sucks." Immediately I was consumed with shock (Why would anyone do such a thing?), outrage (I'll catch this person if it's the last thing I do!), and finally, hurt (What did I do to deserve this?).

I shifted quickly into detective mode and scanned the cafeteria, hoping for a clue, a sign, anything that would lead to the apprehension of the culprit. He would not get away with it . . . not on my watch! It was then that a fellow colleague approached me and asked if anything was wrong. "Wrong?" I asked. "Look at this! I'm giving my heart and soul to these kids, and this is what I get in return?"

Fortunately he was a veteran teacher, and his comments taught me to handle such matters in the future in a more humorous manner. "You have to tip your hat to the guy," he began. "Do you know how hard it is to write that neatly using a squirt bottle? And you at least have to appreciate that he took the time to write 'Mr.' before 'Kitchen.' Even though he thinks you suck, at least he respects you."

This advice taught me a very valuable lesson. I realized that the only way I would survive would be to laugh more often and maintain a sense of humor.

Another example occurred just last fall. I can vividly remember delivering what I thought was an extremely inspirational lecture on the importance of using good grammar in writing—during the final period of the day on a hot Friday afternoon. I had already graded a sample of my students' writing, and, from a grammar standpoint, it was atrocious. I was trying to impress upon them how important it was to take pride in their work and how often they would be judged by the quality of their writing. I was waving my arms, moving from one side of the room to the other, raising and lowering my voice with perfect inflection. I could tell that it was one of those instances when I truly was "making a connection." It didn't matter that it was the last period of the last day of the school week. I had everyone's attention—all eyes were on me. I was at least fifteen minutes into my presentation before I saw the first finger point. Then a snicker. Then a giggle. I was furious! I confronted the offenders immediately. "What is so funny?"

Sheepishly, embarrassingly, the object of my ire replied, "Mr. Kitchen, your zipper is down."

I could have handled this in a variety of ways, but I chose the most honest one: I laughed. In fact, I laughed hysterically, and so did my class. They recognized that I was human, and I demonstrated to them that not only did I have sense of humor, perhaps even more importantly, I was able to laugh at myself. You should, too.

It's well documented that kids learn best from teachers they like. Although you're not out to win your students over as friends, they will look forward to your class if they know you possess a sense of humor and that they might be able to enjoy a laugh or two (sometimes at your expense).

There are going to be times every day when you can either allow yourself to become angry or to simply laugh, and I recommend the latter. Anger will only increase stress levels as well as your blood pressure. It's not worth it! If you can enter your first classroom and be able to laugh occasionally with the kids—sometimes at yourself—you'll be on your way to not just a successful first year, but a successful career in education.

FIVE

Establishing Your Philosophy on Teaching, Grading, Discipline, and Classroom Management

Yet another mistake I made when I first started teaching was the lack of a clear philosophy and plan regarding these topics. Let's first start with establishing your philosophy of education.

TEACHING PHILOSOPHY

Most methods classes in colleges unfortunately are not very practical. Many of the professors who teach these classes have not actually taught in a high school classroom for many years. However, they will often insist that you subscribe to certain principles and tenets regarding philosophy that simply aren't true.

As an example, let's look at a typical philosophy of education: All children can be taught to learn. Sounds pretty reasonable, right? Wrong! First, it's completely untrue. Although everyone *is* capable of learning (I don't dispute this), some individuals might not be during that stage of their life when *your* paths cross. Some teens bring so much emotional baggage from home that, when they come to school, there's no way they could ever learn in your class (or anyone else's), and no matter what you try to do, you can't save them. This goes back to the "Kids are kids" theory. It's a crock! Some kids are so screwed up by the time they reach your class that it might take years of therapy to get them straightened out.

I once had a student who adamantly refused to take notes or offer any type of effort on quizzes or tests. He turned most of them in blank! Despite multiple conferences (one-on-one as well as with guidance counselor and parents), he never wavered. He *chose* to fail. If this happens to you, first try to talk to him one-on-one. If that doesn't help, consult the guidance counselor, who in turn will most likely involve the parent(s). Even if nothing works, you did everything possible to reach this particular student; he obviously has issues that currently preclude him from heeding anyone's advice. Don't take it personally . . . it's not your fault!

If you go into your first year thinking you will be able to save every troubled student, you'll end up as yet another statistic who abandoned the field of education within your first three to five years. It happened to me, and it occurs with hundreds of first-year teachers who believe they can save the world and turn the life around of every troubled child. (And make no mistake about it—every school has its share of troubled students.)

I spent my entire first year trying to encourage all of my students to set high goals, give their best effort, and go to college. Although some listened, others chose a path of apathy. As I mentioned earlier, the year before I arrived, only 10 percent of the high school graduates attended college. Then, at the end of my first year, that figure dropped to 8 percent. Although I might have made minimal progress with a few of the tougher cases, I used nearly all of my energy on them and drained myself well before the end of the school year. Within my first three years of a career in which I had planned to spend my entire working life, I was burned out!

Do you think you'll ever hear in any college class that some kids are going to be beyond your help? No, you definitely won't. Do you think that during a job interview you should tell a building principal or superintendent that, if presented with an extremely challenging student, you will not be able to help him? Absolutely not! No administrator wants to hear that some kids are beyond your help, but it's a fact that you must understand if you plan on making a career out of teaching.

Please understand that although my previous comments probably sound callous, I'm not suggesting you give up on anyone. Do your best with all of your students—but there comes a time when you have to back off and let someone sink (or swim). It's a harsh reality, and admitting it to an administrator during your job interview—or to anyone else, for that matter—will make securing a position virtually impossible, but it's a truth that I wish I'd known when I started.

Even after my explanation, I'm quite certain many of you will still have a difficult time accepting what I just wrote—that's understandable. No aspiring teacher wants to hear that some kids will be impossible to reach. But you don't have to change anything dramatically—just give your philosophy a slight tweak (as I wish I had done before I started my first job). Adopt this mind-set: "I will do my very best with all my students at all times, but in no way can I or will I sacrifice the needs of the entire class for one student. I will make time for anyone who is in need of my help, but there is only so much I can do." You can you live with that, can't you?

I want you to enter your first classroom as a realist and not the ideological "I can save every student who enters my classroom." This philosophy will only lead to disappointment and burnout—that's exactly what happened to me.

DISCIPLINE AND CLASSROOM MANAGEMENT PHILOSOPHY

If you adopt a philosophy like the one I'm recommending, you'll also have a built-in strategy on discipline and classroom management, which pretty much go hand-in-hand. Don't waste time drawing up a bunch of petty classroom rules and consequences—this is not discipline. If you remain cognizant of the fact that you will not allow anyone or anything to prevent you from doing your job—teaching your students—you will have secured the backbone of your discipline and classroom management plan.

If you were planning that first day (and I'll address this again later in much more detail) on bombarding your students with rules such as "If you are late to class, you'll receive a detention," "If you don't do your homework, you'll get a detention," "If you talk when I'm talking, you'll get a detention," you are making a huge mistake. Instead, look directly into their eyes, talk to them in a confident and professional yet noncondescending manner, and verbally deliver your expectations. Tell them that you expect their best effort and that they in turn can expect yours. If students know where they stand on the very first day, you'll have a much better chance of preventing potential discipline problems before they ever begin to surface.

GRADING PHILOSOPHY

After discussing expectations, you then need to explain how you plan to evaluate your students. First, let me explain my theory and why it works for me. Because I'm a very competitive person, I believe that students should expect to be evaluated on a daily basis. Whatever your subject— math, science, history—your kids should be held accountable every day! This makes them feel as if each day in your class is important.

The way I accomplish this is by providing multiple evaluations throughout the term. In fact, at the end of a grading period, my students end up averaging nearly one grade per day. That doesn't necessarily mean that I evaluate students daily; some days, I give two and possibly three quizzes, such as vocabulary, grammar, and spelling, all on the same day. But as all educators would agree, it's easy to administer the quizzes . . . the problem arises when they have to be graded.

My solution is this: I only grade every fourth or fifth quiz myself while the others I have the students grade in class. I either have them pass their papers up or back one person, and as I go over the correct answers the students score them immediately. Occasionally I will collect the graded papers just to make certain they were scored accurately, and 99 percent of the time there are no mistakes.

As an educator, many times you'll realize that you're not just teaching the subject matter, you're often teaching values . . . and this is one of those times. I discuss the importance of being honest and trustworthy at length before we exchange papers the first time of the year, and then I give the students multiple opportunities to demonstrate these two qualities.

Most evaluations are written, but on many occasions I give oral quizzes, especially with vocabulary. I'll simply hold up a word and give the student ample time to respond with the definition. Then I record the score on my computer immediately after the student responds.

Unfortunately, not all educators share a similar philosophy on multiple evaluations. In fact, there will be some teachers on your staff who give their students only a mere handful of grades each quarter. However, I would strongly advise against this practice! These teachers are the ones who inevitably get the most complaints from students as well as parents.

I also utilize a point system, which means I assign a specific point value to every quiz, test, or paper, and at the end of the quarter the computer figures the percentage of points earned compared to the total possible. For example, if a student earns an A+ on a paper, I type in 100 for the points earned on that particular assignment, and immediately the computer updates that individual's overall percentage and letter grade for the term. This enables me to always know what each student's grade is on a daily basis. I previously had to figure this all by hand, but when our school adopted a computerized grading system, it obviously made my job much easier.

As far as final grades are concerned, our school uses the seven-point scale. If a student earns 93 percent of my total points possible for the quarter (and I usually end up with approximately 1,000 points based all on the quizzes, tests, and papers), he receives an A, 85–92 percent equals a B, and so on. As I mentioned earlier, I will evaluate my students thirty-five to forty times (at the minimum) per ten-week grading period, and although some quizzes might only be worth 5–10 points, tests and papers could represent 100–200 points each. This way, every student receives an excellent opportunity to earn the grade for which he is striving, and by providing so many evaluations, one or two poor performances won't ruin anyone's chance for a good overall grade in the class.

In addition, I do a grade check every Friday. This might be extremely time consuming if your school doesn't use a computerized grading system, but I feel it's well worth the time it takes to allow all students to see their exact grade every Friday of each week of the school year. This way, there are no surprises to students or parents when midterms or reports cards are sent. If you didn't know this already, 90 percent of all parent complaints stem from grade issues. By keeping your students and parents updated on a weekly (and for some a daily) basis, several parents who might otherwise be tempted to call to check on their child's progress will abstain, and you won't be burdened with the job of having to return all those calls to explain grades.

Our grading program is called Easy Grade Pro, and it not only adds up totals and figures percentages, it also breaks down a student's average in all categories. For example, in my class, categories include "vocabulary," "spelling," "writing," "literature," and "grammar," and concerned students or parents requesting printouts receive the overall average as well as the exact breakdown of percentages in all categories. (See sample.)

Figure 5.1   Sample Grade Sheet

Student Progress Report, Term 4
Friday, January 16, 2003
Honors English

Doe, John
Overall grade: 92.2% B +

Assignments:

#	Date	Assignment	Score	Points	Grade
1	3/25	Homework	10	15	66.7% F
2	3/27	Vocabulary	10	10	100% A
3	3/28	Spelling	15	15	100% A
4	4/2	Essay	90	100	90% B
5	4/3	Grammar	24	25	96% A
6	4/5	Speech	47	50	94% A
7	4/6	Homework	0	10	0% F
8	4/8	Vocabulary	15	15	100% A
9	4/9	Grammar	32	39	82.1% C
10	4/10	Paragraph	49	50	98% A

Grammar	54/62	87.5%
Vocabulary	25/25	100%
Homework	10/25	40%
Writing	139/150	92.6%
Spelling	15/15	100%
Speech	47/50	94%

Six

Final Thoughts on Preparation

You will find yourself throughout the days, weeks, or months prior to your first day on the job thinking a lot about yourself as an educator and perhaps setting personal and professional goals for your initial teaching assignment. Sure, you'll be nervous, but that's okay. What I've learned over the years is that any time I'm getting ready to do something important, the more time I spend preparing and the more ideas and thoughts I write down, the less anxiety I feel!

Let me say that once again, especially because most individuals *avoid* thinking about what they consider a stressful situation since they don't want to worry more than is necessary. However, by continuing to jot down ideas and thoughts, you are thinking, planning, and preparing for what's to come . . . and the more preparation you put into something, the better your performance will be and the less stress you'll experience when the event actually arrives. Preparation helps to eliminate stress!

Even now, after twenty years of teaching, I'm constantly making lists of what I need to buy, what tasks I need to complete, and what new ideas I'm planning for the upcoming year, and it's not because I'm getting senile. It is the key to my success, and it will work for you.

SEVEN

Twenty-Four Hours and Counting

THE DAY BEFORE

You will most likely have a "work day" the day before classes begin where you might get a free breakfast; you'll hear some introductory remarks from your superintendent, principal, and possibly your board of education president; and you'll spend a large chunk of your day in meetings. You might have some time to work in your room, but it might not be until late in the afternoon.

Although your meetings could help answer some of the last-minute questions, the most important part of this day could occur at lunchtime. Even if you don't know anyone, it's likely somebody will invite you to join his or her group for lunch. Here's my advice: Whoever asks, go! This is an excellent opportunity to socialize with your fellow staff members, and if you remain in the same district for several years, you're likely to make some very close friends. If you heeded my advice on preparation, you shouldn't have any substantial work to complete in your room, so don't put anything ahead of spending some relaxing quality time away from the building on that day with fellow teachers. Then, while you're at lunch, listen! Don't try to add to the conversation unless you're asked. Especially early in the year, whenever you are in a social setting or at a meeting with veteran teachers, *talk less and listen more*.

After the final meeting ends, return to your classroom and make a brief checklist of any final tasks to complete. Then, write your name as well as the starting and ending time for each period—and the lunch schedules—neatly on the board. (This will spare you of all the "What time is this class over?" questions.) If you can't write neatly, then print—first impressions are crucial. Everything on that first day needs to symbolize confidence and professionalism.

Next, get your textbooks ready (if you are lucky enough to have them) and place your first day handout(s) on your desk. Be sure your seating chart for each class is handy, and take the necessary time to print the names of all your students in your grade book or type them on your computer. Try not to stay past 4 or 5 p.m., but before you leave, go over everything one last time—especially your opening remarks, which are covered in chapter 8.

THE NIGHT BEFORE

Throughout your first year of teaching, punctuality should be one of your top priorities. The night before your first day, common sense should tell you to get a good night's rest, but I'm not sure that's possible. If you can spend time with friends or family, I'd recommend it, but I'd also advise getting home early.

Set your alarm—plan on arriving at school at least thirty minutes early each day of your first week—and then get to bed by 11 p.m. (If you have any doubts at all about your alarm, have a friend or family member give you a wake-up call on that first day, just to be sure.) Getting to bed early on this night is probably not going to be as beneficial as it will be in the days or weeks ahead, mainly because nerves can make it difficult for you to get a quality night's sleep.

As I've already stated, there's nothing wrong with being nervous, but you shouldn't be "stressed." Stress is caused by a lack of preparation, both physical and mental. However, because you've prepared diligently since the day you were hired, stress should not be an issue. You've been to your new school many times, and on several occasions you've stood in the front of your classroom and visualized a room full of students. You've repeatedly practiced your opening remarks, your room has been decorated and organized for days (if not weeks), and your name and the starting and ending time for each class are written neatly on the board. Your seating charts are filled out, your desks are organized to your lik-ing, and all of your handouts and textbooks are ready. Your desk is stocked with all the supplies you could possibly need, and you already have your names written in your grade book or typed on your computer. Lesson plans have been made for your first two weeks of classes, and you've also mapped out your general strategy for the first quarter as well as the entire year. Nervous, sure, but stressed—definitely not. You're ready!

THE MORNING OF

Even if you didn't sleep very well, after a good shower you'll be awake and alert. You should eat something for breakfast, even if it's only a bagel, a piece of toast, or a banana. Then, leave home at a time that will enable you to pull into the school parking lot at least a full thirty minutes before your required arrival time . . . you now have ample opportunity to deal with any last-minute problems that may arise. Check your mailbox and retrieve any memos or announcements that will affect or alter your day. Go to your classroom, check to make certain that nothing has been moved, changed, or erased, and make any necessary adjustments. If you still have time—and you probably will—before that first class, go to the lounge and relax. Read the paper or just listen to the conversations. Relax! There's no possible way that you could have prepared any more than you have. You're ready!

Finally, after you return to your room and before you head to your door to greet your students, look in your mirror one final time. I'll never forget being in high school and having a new teacher greet us at the door with part of his breakfast on his chin. (Or even worse, how disgusting would it be to have something hanging out of your nose?) Your final two words before you greet your first class are only intended for your ears and are simple ones, but you must say them out loud and with conviction: "I'm ready."

YOUR FIRST CLASS IS NOW
ONLY MINUTES AWAY

Take your position at the door to welcome your class, and greet everyone with a warm smile and a friendly hello. You'll be amazed at how much you'll immediately be able to ascertain about many of your students just by saying "Hi" or "Good morning" to them.

It's important to get into the habit of doing this, not just on your first day, but every day! Students will enter your room in a much more orderly manner and will normally be punctual if you are standing at your door on a daily basis. In addition, administrators love it when their teachers are at their door or in the hallway . . . it makes their job easier because usually students won't misbehave in the hallways if they see a teacher is watching.

THE MOMENT HAS ARRIVED . . .
YOUR FIRST CLASS BEGINS

Then it happens . . . the bell rings, and suddenly the last few scurry into your room while those who were already inside drop backpacks and plunk down into a desk. You should remain standing at your door momentarily, allowing latecomers a final opportunity to get inside the classroom—*your classroom*—and when they do arrive, don't make a big deal of it on the first day. Although you might have been eagerly awaiting this day for weeks, even months, most of them have been dreading it.

Momentarily, you'll close your door and enter, hoping that each child's eyes are eagerly fixed on your every move . . . and they might be. But remember, the sound of a bell, especially that first one after three months of summer vacation, means nothing to some students. Twenty-four hours ago, most—if not all—of them were sound asleep, so be cognizant of this. Many, even the brightest ones, quite possibly won't be in any mood to share your enthusiasm on that first day.

Before sealing off the rest of the world from your own personal domain for the next fifty minutes, stand in the hallway for a brief moment. Take a deep breath, and gain your composure. You're a professional educator!

From this point on, there is no way to predict exactly what's going to happen next, but it's one of the many things you'll come to love about teaching. As trite as it might sound, every day is indeed different. However, I am going prepare you for what could happen, from the best-case scenario to the worst one, so that hopefully very little will surprise you. And remember, whatever does happen that first day, deal with it as a learning experience. If you truly love working with children and you are willing to heed my advice when applicable, you stand an excellent chance of reaching your potential as an educator.

EIGHT

How to Begin and What You Should Say to Your First Class

As previously mentioned, no first-year teacher will survive without becoming a master of classroom management and discipline techniques. But first, I want to define what these terms actually mean to you. As far as classroom management is concerned, you simply have to make what one of my students once referred to as a "presence." Even if you don't feel as confident on your very first day as you would like, you will definitely make a presence by speaking with sincerity and poise.

DON'T DO THIS!

Although mastering effective classroom management skills is a lengthy and ongoing process, those initial few days and weeks are crucial. However, before I begin with some effective strategies, I first want to make you aware of two techniques that you should avoid. In fact, using either of these will lead to failure and quite possibly preclude you from even surviving until Thanksgiving.

The first negative technique is what I call the "Drill Sergeant Power-Trip Method." A teacher who subscribes to this theory (and I was one of them) walks into class on day one with the ultimate goal of making certain that all students realize unequivocally that he is in charge, and that his opinion is the only one that counts. His theory is "All students will do as I say . . . or else."

39

Although I certainly advocate that you be strict with your students, especially during those initial few days and weeks, you must also be compassionate and somewhat sympathetic. What will ultimately occur in the classroom of these "power-trippers" is that their students will not only defy them—at times, intentionally—but they will drive these misguided educators right out of teaching. The only way this method can be effective is if the teacher first earns the students' respect, and this occurs only over time. You must start out being firm but fair, but most importantly, honest. As was discussed earlier, the first step is to explain your expectations and be sure your students know that above all else your job is to help them be successful. If they feel they know you and can trust you, you'll stand a much greater chance of being an effective leader.

Thirty years ago, teachers could get by with this "hard-ass" approach because the respect factor for teachers was innate. Now, however, you must earn it, and if you attempt to rule without first gaining respect, you are doomed for failure. Even then, if they respect you, will they still test you? Absolutely. Will they test you on that very first day? Maybe. But as long as you're not obsessed with the power aspect of the teaching profession, you'll find it much easier to handle trouble in a more effective and efficient manner.

The second technique that many rookie teachers erroneously adopt is what I call "The Buddy System." These teachers enter the classroom thinking they will be friends with their students. They feel that if they get their kids to like them, they will be better teachers with fewer discipline problems. This is another huge mistake. Unfortunately, sooner or later, the "I want to be my students' buddy" type of teachers realize that they must tighten up the reins on their class because the students don't respect them . . . unfortunately, by then, it's too late!

A veteran female teacher at one of my former schools enters class every year on her first day and proclaims, "I am a bitch. I am not here to be your friend. I am your teacher, and if you choose to pay attention, you will learn. If not, you are wasting my time and yours, and I will have no choice but to remove you from my room." Although I wouldn't ever recommend introducing yourself as a "bitch," the rest of her opening day remarks are very appropriate. But keep in mind, she is a veteran teacher, and this approach works for her.

You are not being paid to be friends with your students! Eventually you will foster relationships with many of your kids, but early on, you should not even be thinking about becoming anyone's friend.

AN EFFECTIVE METHOD OF ESTABLISHING A PRESENCE ON YOUR FIRST DAY

After that final bell sounds, indicating the start of first period, walk confidently to your desk and sit on the edge of it. As nervous as you might be on that first day (and I'll say it again—it's okay to be nervous), standing could potentially be a big problem. Remember, you don't want to have any distracting habits that will preclude students from focusing on what you're saying. For example, when you talk in front of people, do you sway? Fidget? Play with your hair? On this day, your public speaking skills need to be at their best, so as you begin to deliver your opening day remarks, unless you're extremely relaxed and confident, sit on the edge of your desk! Sitting should hopefully help eliminate any nervous distractions, and at the same time, it sends a subtle message to your students that you are talking to them instead of lecturing.

Your tone should be compassionate, yet also sober and sincere. If you feel the need to stand up and move after you have started, do so, but deliver your opening remarks from a comfortable position. Remember that when you are standing *above* your students, that in itself symbolizes power . . . you are "over" them. However, if you meet them "halfway"—sitting on your desk—you're still over them, but neither your position nor your voice will send that "I'm on a power trip" message that I referred to earlier.

Okay, you've taken your place (on the edge of your desk), and your class looks like they are going to give you the benefit of the doubt as all eyes are on you, awaiting your first words. As the school year progresses, the first thing you'll do each class is take attendance . . . but not on the first day. You still might get additional students, whether they are new to the school or simply from a schedule change. These will only create those distractions that could easily have been avoided had you put off taking attendance until later in the period.

HANDLING DISTRACTIONS

Before I give you the specifics of what I recommend you say to your very first class, let's start by dealing with distractions. No matter what might happen on your first day, distractions are unavoidable. Remembering to close your door can eliminate some of them—it's extremely chaotic and noisy in the hallways on the first day at any school. In addition, a closed door could also keep out the assistant principal or the veteran teacher next door who wants to drop in to check on you, and it could prevent a surprise visit from the guidance counselor, who might be looking for a particular student to change a schedule. A closed door usually means you're busy, and you hope these potential "momentum busters" will leave you alone, at least until the end of the period.

Unfortunately, morning announcements on the P.A. system and late arrivers (some of whom might be new to your school) are often inevitable, so be prepared. Again, greet any new students in a warm, friendly manner and courteously listen to the announcements, but then immediately resume whatever you were doing or saying. Extended distractions invite students to begin talking, and you don't want this, especially on your first day.

STEP #1: LET THEM KNOW
YOUR EXPECTATIONS

Start by welcoming everyone back and letting them know that you hope they had a good summer. Then, introduce yourself, point to the schedule already written on the board, and let everyone know what time the class officially begins and ends. Now it's time to talk about expectations, which are a crucial part of establishing sound discipline and classroom management practices.

Classroom management and discipline problems are often the result of unclear expectations on the teacher's part. If kids know where you stand and why you feel the way you do, most will not cross that line. I am not saying you still won't get tested—I'll address that shortly—but you will most likely get the benefit of the doubt, especially that first day, if you let your students know where they stand. I also think it's important to first let the kids know what they can expect from you. Most teachers do just the opposite, and so students often automatically feel less important than their teachers. By telling them what they can expect from you first, you are recognizing *their* worth, and again, they won't feel like you are talking down to them.

As soon as you inform your students what time the class begins and ends (and you should say it, even though it's written on the board), I recommend saying the following:

> Before I tell you about this class and what we'll be doing this year, I first want you to understand my expectations of you, as well as what you can expect from me. I'm going to begin with what you can expect from me. My job is to help each and every one of you learn and be successful in this class, and I'm willing to work with any of you before or after school if you need extra help. As you might know, this is my first teaching job, and I'm really looking forward to it. I feel very fortunate to be your teacher, and I hope that no matter what experience you've had with [name of your subject] in the past, you will at least give this class—and me—a chance. If you ever don't understand something or you feel totally lost, please know that you can always ask questions during class, or as I said, you can come to me outside of class. I can't emphasize enough that I'm here to help you. [pause] Now let me say that again. My job, first and foremost, is to help you learn [name of subject]. You should also know that I'm not a big fan of piling on homework, but I am big on effort, so when I do assign homework, I expect it to be done.
>
> Other than effort, I have only two additional expectations of you, but each of these is vitally important. First, when I'm talking, you listen. This is a big one with me, and if you can't abide by this rule, you are preventing me from doing my job, and I won't let you do that . . . this job and all of you mean too much to me. The consequences will be that you'll end up in the hall or the office.
>
> Second, I want to deal with the respect issue. Although I'm not going to tell you that you have to respect me, you do have to respect each other. If you violate this rule, there will be no argument or discussion . . . you will simply be asked to leave the class. As far as respecting me is concerned, I hope that in the coming days and weeks I can earn your respect. Now, are there any questions concerning expectations?

If you receive any questions, answer them honestly. If anyone asks about specifics related to the class, such as grading procedures, defer your answers until later in the period. Then, when there are no more questions, say, "Okay, it's now time for me to start learning names and assigning seats."

Analysis

Let's take a quick look at what you just said and why you said it, but I hope that based on many of my previous comments in earlier chapters you already know the answers. First of all, you are being honest and forthright with your class, and you are not imposing several petty rules that most kids don't want to hear, especially on that first day. You've told them exactly where they stand, and you've also made it very clear that your main job is to help them. And if the notion that you weren't on any kind of power trip hasn't already sunk in with them, you've driven it clearly home by telling them that although you demand they respect one another, you plan on *earning* their respect.

STEP #2: TAKE ATTENDANCE

Read the names from your seating charts and have each student move to the appropriate desk. Let me warn you: There will be grumbling . . . many of the kids you put in the front won't want to be there. However, many of the decisions that you make (even concerning seating arrangements) are not going to be popular ones, but they don't have to be; you are their teacher, not their friend. Just maintain your sense of humor and laugh off any remarks. Be sure to pronounce everyone's name correctly and record any changes (e.g., "Bill" instead of "William").

Once everyone is in place, inform your students that this will be their seat until further notice. Again, as soon as this announcement is made, be prepared for some additional unfavorable remarks. Expect it! If anyone is really persistent in wanting to be in a different seat location, buy some time by saying, "We'll see how things go for a while, and possibly, if all of you behave, I'll consider making some changes in a few weeks." Then, get back to business.

STEP #3: DISTRIBUTE TEXTBOOKS,
YOUR LETTER, GRADING INFORMATION,
AND SYLLABUS

As soon as everyone is where you want them, hand out the textbooks. Then give students a 3" × 5" card and ask them to record their name, the number of the textbook, and any rips, tears, loose bindings, and so forth. I always recommend covering all textbooks, and I normally offer extra credit to get them covered by the end of that first week of school. Next, collect the cards and file them away (you probably won't need them again until the end of the year).

Now it's time to give each student a copy of the letter of introduction you prepared for parents (see figure 2.1). Even though a percentage of these will never make it home, those that do will immediately create a favorable impression with the parents . . . and this is extremely important. Those who chose to attend Open House (also referred to as "Back-to-School Night") will already feel like they know you.

Then, distribute information regarding grading procedures (figure 2.3) and go over it carefully. Answer any questions, and then hand out your syllabus (figure 2.2), which includes only a brief overview of the first quarter. Avoid getting too specific on any document that goes home, especially concerning dates . . . always allow for adjustments and flexibility in your planning. Just provide enough information to let them know where they are headed.

If you don't finish covering all of this information on the first day, it's okay! Or, if you want to stop a little early because you somehow finished ahead of one of your other classes, do it. You could then complete the discussion of your syllabus tomorrow. Don't get overly concerned with meeting personal deadlines—this is a brand new experience for you! When you do your lesson plans (more about this later), always allow 1 to 2 days of "flex" time just in case you have distractions that prevent you from finishing something on time (e.g., pep rally, assembly, fire drill, students struggling with the material, etc.). This way, if you do finish on schedule or even ahead of time, fine, but if not, you're prepared.

STEP #4 (OPTIONAL): TELL THEM THEY CAN
ASK YOU QUESTIONS ABOUT YOUR LIFE
OUTSIDE OF SCHOOL

I've always been a firm believer in being honest with kids (to a certain extent) and allowing them to see me as a real person. I do not hesitate to talk about my family, my background, my hobbies, and so on. However, if you don't feel comfortable doing so, skip this step.

Whether you decide to complete step #4 or not, at the end of each class on that first day, take a few minutes to talk with your students, especially those you consider to be potential troublemakers. You might wonder how you could possibly tell who the problems are in just one class period, but in many cases, even without previous warnings from other teachers, you'll know almost immediately when they enter your classroom. Most of these types of kids are looking for a stage and an audience, and school gives them both. Each year, I ask the guidance counselors to provide me with some background information on the so-called troublemakers that I will have in my classes. Then, once I discover a hobby or interest these students have outside of school, I'll use this to establish some sort of rapport.

A few years ago, I had several teachers as well as the assistant principal warn me about a particular boy who, during his previous year, had spent almost as much time out of school (on suspension) as he had in actual classes. I immediately put a plan into action. First, I went to his guidance counselor to see if there was any information that I could use. I learned that his grandmother was raising him, his dad had run off when he was a baby, his mom was an alcoholic, he'd told a teacher to "fuck off," he was caught with marijuana in his backpack, and so on. Unfortunately, this information didn't help. However, on his student interest sheet he had listed soccer as one of his hobbies, so next, I went to talk to the soccer coach—he had no knowledge of this student ever playing. But then I decided to call the previous soccer coach (who was no longer in our district), and not only did he remember my student, he told me the kid was extremely talented—he just couldn't follow team rules (big surprise, right?).

As soon as he entered my class on that first day of school, I immediately pulled him aside and informed him that I needed his help. I told him I had a soccer-related question and that I'd speak to him about it after class. (As far as sports are concerned, I've played and coached baseball and basketball, but I don't know much about soccer, and both of my daughters play on teams.)

During the final three minutes of class, I went to his desk and let him know that I'd heard he was a pretty talented soccer player. I told him about my daughters and asked him if he could explain to me what skills I should be working with them on at home and if he'd come in after school one day and show me the correct way to teach them. I'm not sure any teacher had ever asked this kid's opinion on anything prior to that very moment. Then, not only did he come after school the following day and answer all my questions, we talked about soccer at least once or twice a week throughout the first few months of school . . . and I never had a single discipline problem with him all year! Communication is the key!

NINE

What If Things Aren't Going as Planned?

INITIAL COMMENTS REGARDING DISCIPLINE AND CLASSROOM MANAGEMENT

Many of you might breeze through all four steps on that first day, with everything going exactly as planned; it's not likely, but it's certainly possible. However, one thing is for certain: If your first day is better than you could have ever expected, the second day probably won't be. And the third day could be even worse. But if you read this next section carefully and employ my strategies, you'll at least be prepared for what could possibly happen inside your classroom those first few days. And when you're tested—and you *will* be tested—you'll deal with the adversity in a professional manner and get on with what's most important . . . teaching.

So how about the trouble you may encounter? Suppose the following scenario occurs: The bell sounds and you close your door. You walk confidently across the front of the classroom and take a seat on the edge of your desk just like I recommended. There's only one problem. Just as you're ready to utter your first words as a professional educator, you look around and realize that no one responded to the bell or to the announcements. In fact, as you look out at your class, the noise level hasn't diminished a single decibel. Suddenly your emotional state is shifting into panic mode. You think to yourself, "Holy crap! What's going on? This can't be! Don't they understand that I'm ready to begin? Don't they know that this is the most important day of my life? Don't these kids have any sense of decency?"

My advice to you quite simply is this: Don't feel sorry for yourself! This is an opportunity you are going to seize! Let me explain. As I said earlier, your initial plan was to first introduce yourself, be sure everyone knows what time the class begins and ends, and then start discussing expectations. But not now! No one is listening! It would be a complete waste of energy on your part. However, you can't afford to panic, for this could be the best thing that happens to you on your first day. That's right—the best thing! If your students choose to ignore the bell on that very first day, make this work to your advantage.

Start by getting up off your desk and going to your predetermined spot in the room (mine is behind my lectern). In a firm voice, but without yelling, say, "Okay, class has started; I need your attention, please." Depending on the district and the type of kids, this might be enough. But even if that doesn't work, there's still no need to begin ranting or raving.

So what's your next move? The students have ignored your polite request to be quiet. Should you now get angry and tell them to "shut up?" Or are you going to again politely ask if you can have their attention? Or, even better, are you going to go ahead and start class hoping that the students will automatically quiet down and listen to you? None of these!

This is your chance, as a professional educator, as the leader of your class, to secure a firm grip on the reins of your team of students, and you're going to capitalize on it.

At this point, one thing is certain: The nice approach is not working. You now need to adopt a little bit of attitude. What I mean by that is to shift into your "Knock this crap off; it's time to get started" mode. My standard line is—and always has been—in a raised voice that is loud enough for everyone to clearly hear me, the following: "Hey, that was the bell! When it rings, you have one job: Close your mouths and listen. It's my time, now." When I say this, I make sure my tone is one that is firm, authoritative, and slightly angry.

As odd as this sounds, some of you might need to practice sounding somewhat mean. If you think it is going to be difficult for you to get mad so early on the first day of your teaching career—especially because for so many of you this isn't your true personality—you'd better practice and be prepared. If you can't gain the attention of your class, you can't teach them.

Your classroom is not a democracy! You are in charge, and you have a very important message to deliver. If your students are not willing to listen to you, then they are interfering with the learning process, and if you want to remain as an educator in that school district for any length of time, you must maintain order if any teaching/learning is to take place. Thus, you'd better make it clear to your students on day one that when you talk, they need to listen or they will not be permitted to remain in your class.

This pivotal moment might come only minutes into your very first class. But don't underestimate its significance. You are going to be tested at some point . . . expect it, and then deal with it!

If you are one of those extremely soft-spoken individuals who simply cannot speak loudly enough to be heard over twenty-five chatty adolescents, you'd better improvise . . . drop your garbage can on the floor, flick the lights on and off, or pound a book on your desk. You can't continue until you gain everyone's attention.

There. You now have all eyes on you, and at least for the moment, everyone is quiet. What you say now is crucial, especially because for the first time in the period—and in your career—you are in charge. Here's what you need to say next, again in a *firm and serious tone*:

> Guys, this is my first day of a career I've been working toward for the last four years of my life, and I need your cooperation. I'm not a big rules person, but there are a couple we have to have in order to function. The first one is this: When the bell rings, that means class has started, and when I'm talking, you listen. If you talk when I'm talking, you're preventing me from doing my job, and I'm not going to allow you to do that . . . this job and all of you mean too much to me. [pause] Let me say that again . . . this job and all of you [point to your class] mean too much to me. And the consequences are easy ones as far as I'm concerned. Follow this rule, or you'll end up in the hall or the office. Second, and finally, is the issue of respect. I'm not going to tell you that you have to respect me, but you do have to respect each other. If someone raises his hand and is speaking, everyone—including me—will listen. As far as respecting *me* is concerned, I hope that in the coming days and weeks I can *earn* your respect. Are there any questions?

There probably won't be, so wait only about three seconds and then immediately say, "Okay, now it's time for me to start learning names and assigning seats."

Only the mental midgets or social misfits/outcasts will act out now because you've been firm but fair, terse but compassionate. However, if someone does, here's your next move. Whether it's while you're taking attendance or afterward, if someone now has the audacity to test you further, deal with it. I will always, at least on the first day, try a little humor at this point because I realize that if someone is going to cause any more trouble for a new teacher on his first day—especially after you just told the entire class twice how much they all mean to you—this person can't be very intelligent. However, be prepared to handle it . . . this way, nothing will surprise you!

If this situation does occur, look the student directly in the eyes, and say, "[Student's name], right? You look like a pretty intelligent person." (You're obviously lying, but he doesn't know that. In fact, you might be the first person who has ever referred to him as intelligent.) "I really need you to work with me on this. Do you think you could please allow me to finish what I have to say? You'll at least cooperate with me on my first day, won't you? Cause all the trouble you want tomorrow . . . I'll gladly kick you out of here tomorrow, but let's get along today, okay? Thanks."

In 99.9 percent of all cases, this will be enough and you'll be able to continue on with your opening day remarks. However, if the student persists in being a problem, your next course of action is to say, "[Name of student], I've tried my best, but for now, please wait out in the hall until the end of class." He'll most likely go willingly, but you're not dealing with a genius here, so he still might complain, whine, or even mutter some obscenities in your direction. If he insults or threatens you in any way, immediately say, "[Name of student], go to the office." Never tolerate a student using profanity toward you or making threats.

Then, if you do send a student to the office, this is now an assistant principal matter. As soon as class ends, find your assistant principal and tell him or her exactly what happened. If the administration does not deal with this matter and punish the offender severely, then unfortunately, you might have chosen the wrong district in which to teach. You'll soon come to realize that the school is only as strong as its teachers and administrators, and good administrators always support their teachers. If you don't feel supported, don't remain in that district any longer than one year. Don't be naive enough to believe that there aren't better districts than the one in which you're currently teaching.

Analysis

You just accomplished a lot of very important things that sometimes take new teachers an entire year to learn. Unfortunately, many quit the profession early in their careers because they never figure them out. The first important piece of information you gave to your class was that you were not a "rules person." That's a definite plus for you because most teens have had countless teachers who have dozens of rules with specific punishments for each. For example, late to class, one detention; talking out of turn, two detentions; writing on desks, two detentions; etc. Kids don't want to hear all about the petty stuff—at least not on the first day. You can easily say to them at the end of class that the school has specific rules governing, for example, tardiness, and if you're late to class the school policy is that you'll receive a detention.

The second lesson you taught your class was that you are not going to ignore unacceptable behavior. Many teachers—especially new ones—will simply hope that the bad behavior goes away. Not you. A student continued to act out, and you gave him more than one chance (which, by the way, you won't do any more). You stopped what you were doing, looked him in the eyes, and let him know without embarrassing him that you needed his cooperation because you had a job to do and nothing was going to prevent you from doing it.

Yet another mistake I made my rookie year was to immediately re-move a troublemaker on that very first day. I wanted everyone to know that I was in charge, and although my reasoning might have been sound, my actions were foolish. All I ended up doing was alienating a student within minutes of meeting him as well as sending the message that I was one of those power-tripping new teachers.

Being firm and being an insensitive, power-hungry jerk are two com-pletely different things. As I've already discussed, don't get obsessed with your power. But being assertive, firm, authoritative, and raising your voice, not to the point of screaming, but where you're staking your claim to the ownership of your classroom, is imperative.

Finally, you let everyone know that you had a sense of humor, which, as you know by now, is undoubtedly one of the most important qualities a teacher can possess. You stated that you'd gladly throw a student out of class tomorrow, but on the very first day you'd really appreciate it if he'd cooperate.

So, now your class recognizes that you are serious about your job, you aren't going tolerate potential troublemakers, you aren't on a power trip, you have a sense of humor, and perhaps most importantly, *you are in control.*

TEN

Disciplining Your Students:
React, but Don't Overreact

You certainly need some type of plan and philosophy (as I discussed earlier), but there is no way to adequately prepare for every possible discipline situation that you'll encounter. For example, it's easy to have a rule that clearly states a student will receive a detention for being late. However, does that mean that if a student is in the doorway—but not in his seat—when the bell rings, he is, by your definition, late? And what if a student claims he was tardy because he had to use the restroom? What if he couldn't get his locker door open? What if he was assisting a physically handicapped student when the bell rang? Which of these instances warrants a detention?

You must have flexibility and creativity when dealing with today's teenagers. While many would oppose a theory that embraces treating each circumstance differently, you cannot go strictly "by the book" when dealing with discipline. Some would argue, "You must treat everyone the same and show no favoritism." Let me cite an example, and you decide what should have been done.

Shortly after the rash of violence invaded our schools in the 1990s (Columbine, Paducah, Jonesboro), a school in our area adopted a Zero Tolerance Policy. It stated the following:

> Any student who engages in violent, disruptive, or inappropriate behavior shall be subject to the discipline procedures set forth in the student code of conduct for violations of that code. Included in this prohibition would be threats of violent acts of physical harm such as written or verbal

55

threats, hit lists, or any listing of student or faculty names with implied
threats, false alarms, etc., even under the guise of a joke.

After the policy was in place, an interesting situation occurred. Most
schools hold elections every year for student government, where the
student body has the right of voting for such offices as class president,
vice-president, secretary, and so on. The week before the elections, can-
didates normally post signs around school to hopefully drum up support
and win votes. Sometime during the week before the elections, the top-
ranked student in the senior class, who wasn't running for any office,
made a sign for his girlfriend, who was running. He posted it in the boys'
restroom, inside the door of one of the stalls, and it read, "There is a
bomb underneath this toilet seat. If you don't promise to vote for [girl-
friend's name] for class president, when you get up, this toilet will explode."

Can you guess what happened? The boy who prepared the sign was
suspended for violating the Zero Tolerance Policy, and this touched off
a major controversy in the community. However, the administration
held firm, and the suspension was upheld. There was local and even
national news coverage concerning the incident.

If you were the superintendent, what would you have done? Everyone obviously knew the toilet was not going to explode, but according
the policy, he had clearly violated its terms. This is precisely what I
mean when I advise you to sometimes look at the individual circumstances as opposed to enforcing every rule in a literal manner.

Let me further explain some additional discipline situations that I encountered, and then consider how, if faced with similar circumstances,
you would have reacted.

I can vividly remember my first few weeks of teaching, and I also
remember the one piece of valid information I was given about discipline: "It's easier to loosen the reins than it is to tighten them." Have
you heard the same thing? As a result, I was determined that I was going
to assert myself as a staunch disciplinarian from day one. I established
strict rules, and either students abided by them or else. (Sounds like the
classic example of someone on a power trip, right?) The first two weeks
went smoothly—that is until first period on day eleven of my teaching
career. Up until that time, virtually no one had challenged my authority.

And then along came Jake. At the very end of class that particular morn-ing, I committed an egregious error that could have led to a serious situ-ation. In fact, what I did was inexcusable.

Before I go any further, I need to remind you that my first district was very rural—the two major sources of entertainment during the fall, spring, and summer were the drive-in and the roller rink. It was not uncommon to see black eyes and bruised faces on Monday mornings as a result of pugilistic boys doing battle over girls or manhoods being challenged. At 6'0 and 165 pounds, I was hardly an imposing figure, but I was the teacher, right? No student would challenge a teacher, would he?

Here's how the situation unfolded: During the final few minutes of class that morning, my students had started a short reading assignment that I had given for homework—everyone, that is, except Jake. He was busy tearing up little bits of paper and conveniently discarding them onto the floor—my floor. I reacted instantly and foolishly. I confronted him, ordering him to stop and pick up the litter. After his initial shock of being confronted wore off, he simply glared at me. It was one of those "What the hell are you going to do about it if I don't want to?" kind of looks. The entire class was now mesmerized by this confrontation of country giant (Jake was a 6'0, 220-pound freshman that any football coach would have drooled over, but he didn't even play sports) versus scrawny rookie English teacher. I froze. No one had yet challenged my authority, and when it hadn't happened the first day—or even the first week—I naively thought that I was the exception to the "Sooner or later, your authority will be challenged" rule. My attitude up until that point was that teaching wasn't nearly as difficult as everyone had warned it would be.

I then repeated my admonishment, but the tag I added was what could very easily have gotten me into serious trouble. "Jake, you either pick up that paper or . . ." I was stupefied. Or what? What could I possi-bly do? I had now entered into the "wish I hadn't said that" zone. But it was too late. Jake looked defiantly at me . . . there was no way he was going to give in. For a few painful seconds, I honestly had no idea what was the right thing to do. I couldn't physically grab his arm and force him to pick up those few scraps of paper, but I couldn't simply let it go either. I suddenly felt my entire reputation was at stake right there in front of twenty-four adolescents and the man-child (Jake).

Fortunately for me, two good things happened that perhaps saved me . . . and possibly my career. First, the bell rang signifying the end of the period. That enabled me to think about what was happening and to quickly shift into a damage control mode. As the class quickly filed out, with Jake still seated at his desk, I said to him, "We need to go to the office." I didn't say it in a threatening tone; I wanted this confrontation to end. As I walked toward the door, away from Jake's desk, I wasn't sure if he would follow me or not, but he did. He ended up serving three days of detention, and I learned never again to back a student into a corner by delivering a foolish ultimatum.

Another mistake I made involving a discipline problem came one afternoon in the spring of my first year. I remember it was the spring because it involved one of my baseball players (I was the varsity baseball coach). On a literature test over a novel we had just completed (*Great Expectations* . . . remember Pip?), I had marked an answer wrong because Randy, a student in my class and my starting catcher on the baseball team, had misspelled a character's name. After I had passed back the test and we began going over the correct answers, when we reached the fill-in-the-blanks section, Randy's hand immediately went up. I vividly remember being annoyed at his demeanor as he asked the question, because he had one of those "Why are you picking on me?" tones in his voice. (Keep in mind that even though his answer was correct, he had misspelled it, which according to my rules—that had been clearly stated on numerous occasions—meant he received no credit for his answer.) His exact words were as follows: "How can you mark this wrong when I had the correct answer?"

My exact reply, being the first year "I'm on a power trip hard-ass teacher" was, "It's very simple, Randy. I take my pen and make a big, red X."

There are going to be times in your teaching career—whether it's your first year or your twentieth—when you simply allow yourself to slip into a bad mood. Perhaps it's the kids in a certain class, possibly it's a personal problem that carries over into your classroom, or just maybe you don't feel well on a particular day. Whatever the case, it's these days when you have to work your hardest at classroom management and discipline strategies, because a minor confrontation can easily become a full-blown situation—like this one did.

In fact, I made the same error with Randy that I did with Jake, and you need to learn from these mistakes. As difficult as it may be, you must always try your hardest to eliminate anger from the equation when it comes to discipline. You must also learn to take at least a few seconds and think before you act. Remember, even though timing is important in most discipline matters, if you feel that you are becoming angry over what is occurring, pause, maintain your composure, and think before you respond.

All eyes in that room will be on you, and whether you act (or perhaps I should say "overreact") quickly and often foolishly, or whether you pause, even for just a few seconds before you speak, and then act prudently, is totally under your control. Had I just hesitated for a brief couple of seconds before responding, I could have kept the confrontation with Randy a relatively minor one. I should have said, "Randy, I specifically told you that if you misspell a character's name, you will not receive any credit for your answer. I understand you're upset, but I did tell everyone that, didn't I?"

This is another excellent strategy that I like to use, and you should utilize it as well. If a student tries to put you on the spot, the best way to put him in his place is to shift the emphasis away from "you versus him" to the "entire class versus him." You see, because I was certain that I had informed the class about the "no credit for a misspelled answer" rule way before the test was even taken, I should have shifted the attention and the question to the rest of the class, knowing full well that everyone (or at least a large number of students) would concur with me. Instead, I reacted foolishly and took the "hard-ass" approach, which never works.

After I sarcastically said to him that I just take my pen and mark the X, I really didn't help ease the tension; instead, I only exacerbated it, and Randy lost his temper. He immediately shot back, "Well, that's a bunch of shit!" He ended up being suspended from school, and because I chose to play "tough guy," I lost the respect of a good student, a quality person, and my starting catcher.

ELEVEN

Specific Discipline Problems and How to Handle Them

FIGHTING

I've been extremely lucky with this one. In twenty-one years of teaching, I've only been forced to contend with three fights inside my classroom. When dealing with this problem, remember that in most cases, one of the brawlers (and sometimes both) don't really want to fight. Earlier in my career, if a fight broke out, I would rush to intervene . . . that is, until I witnessed a fellow teacher catch a left hook flush on the jaw. Now, I encourage students to help me break up the skirmish, and usually I will go after the smaller of the two and let three or four other students take the big one. High school fights usually don't last much longer than a shove or two and maybe a punch, but you still have to act. Just don't be in an immediate rush to jump in the middle of anything, unless in your professional opinion a student is in danger of being seriously injured because of a physical mismatch.

Many potential fights are often prevented by the presence of teachers in the hallways between classes. Also, just by listening and observing what's going on in your classroom before and at the end of class, you can prevent many potential skirmishes.

Here's an example of how I handled what could have resulted in a fistfight: One day, right before my public speaking class began, I overheard two male students hurling verbal barbs at one another. In any high school, guys are notorious for "ripping on" each other, but in this case, the more I observed, the more heated it became. And then I heard the key phrase, "We'll see," from one of the participants. This type of expression should tell you that the problem has not been resolved and could potentially escalate.

Once class started and various students began getting up and delivering their speeches, the confrontation at least temporarily subsided. Thus, I had about forty-five minutes to devise a strategy to diffuse what I considered to be a pending situation. I knew one of the participants was a football player, so I wrote a note to the football coach, sealed it in an envelope, and I instructed the player involved to deliver the note to his coach and await a response. He had no idea the note concerned him, and it read,

Dear Coach Smith:
  Steve is about to get into a fight with John Taylor. I thought you'd want to know so that you could talk to him.

My message was terse, but it worked out perfectly! Coach Smith spoke to him, and when Steve returned to my class for the final few minutes, he kept his mouth shut and there was no more trouble. Later, Coach Smith thanked me for allowing him to get involved.

Unfortunately, the subject of gangs, guns, knives, and any other weapon has to be broached, especially in connection with fighting or potential violence in the classroom. If you see or suspect any of your students carrying any type of weapon, discreetly send a student to the office with a note for the assistant principal or the principal. If, however, a student pulls out a knife or gun in the midst of an altercation, you have a serious situation that you must at least attempt to handle until help arrives. It disturbs me tremendously that I would have to risk my life, thereby possibly leaving my own children fatherless, to protect someone else's child, but it's our job as teachers to defend our students. Your school will most likely have a plan in place and possibly even offer an in-service day to deal with a situation of this magnitude, but the only thing you really can do is try to remain calm and do the best you can. Easier said than done, right? Do you think you could stay calm if a disgruntled student drew a gun on you or your class? No one can rehearse for such a moment, but you and I both know it could happen. Again, staying under control and reasonably calm could save lives . . . including your own.

STUDENTS MAKING FUN OF
OTHER STUDENTS

Kids of all ages can be extremely cruel to one another. Columbine stirs up painful memories of kids who claimed they were ridiculed and ostracized by "jocks" and other school groups. Teasing is a very real part of high school, but it's your job to know when it's gone too far, and if you're ever in doubt, end it!

I once had a group of students who chose to belittle a peer for the poor quality and brand of jacket he was wearing. I was enraged! But before acting, I sent the child who was being teased on an errand to the office, and then I let the offenders know this would be not be tolerated . . . ever! I wasn't very tactful in my remarks, but I needed to make an immediate point to end this type of ridicule, for it can cause serious emotional harm to weaker students.

Most of this behavior usually occurs at the beginning or end of class—when there is "down time"—and if you pay attention to what is going on in your room, you'll be able to discern when it is occurring and then eliminate it.

TALKING BACK OR BEING DISRESPECTFUL

Why some teachers allow this to go on is incomprehensible to me. Kids will only talk back or be disrespectful if you allow them the opportunity. However, these offenses are serious and cannot be tolerated. Immediately send the student either out in the hall or to the office.

If this behavior does occur in your room, this is exactly what you say, maintaining a tone that is calm and nonthreatening: "[Name of student], you need to go to the office." This should take care of it, but if the student doesn't leave, repeat it in a more authoritative tone: "[Name of student], I said go to the office." If this doesn't work, immediately call for the assistant principal. In the interim, maintain your composure and resume teaching your class—assuming, of course, the student doesn't continue to be a disruption. If he does, simply give the class a brief assignment of some sort until your assistant principal arrives.

Whether he leaves willingly or not, you've just sent the message to the rest of the students that this type of behavior will not be tolerated. The word will get around, and now, other students will know that they can't get away with this in your class. Most kids who will talk back or who are disrespectful need a stage to perform and gain attention. If you eliminate the stage by removing the student from your class, the troublemaker now not only has nowhere to perform, but even more importantly, he has no audience.

Teaching is largely about respect, and if you treat your students in a respectful manner, in most cases they will reciprocate. But if not, take action! If you allow it to continue, more and more students will attempt to use your classroom for their own personal stage.

APATHY

Unfortunately, there's no getting around this one. Whether it's coming from parents or simply from the mind of a confused teenager, apathy will inevitably exist to some extent in your classroom. Remember the basic concept that relates directly back to your teaching philosophy: You can't save everyone. Teach your students to the very best of your ability, but no matter how talented an educator you might be, don't count on reaching everyone. The hardest lesson for doctors to learn is that they can't save all their patients . . . and neither can teachers. And as difficult as it might be and as miserable and helpless as you might feel, don't take it personally. It's not your fault! Many others in your classroom need you and will appreciate what you do for them.

BEING IRRESPONSIBLE AND/OR DISORGANIZED

Thousands of teenagers (probably millions) are extremely irresponsible, and just as many have limited organizational skills. If your students are not properly equipped with supplies, you'll be very limited in what you can teach. However, as the year progresses, you'll come to know those who habitually forget books, pencil, paper, homework, and similar items, and you have to decide on a course of action that you feel comfortable with. I normally have plenty of writing utensils and paper in my room, but I impose a penalty (detention) for those who habitually forget textbooks. On the overall scheme of discipline matters, don't ever let this become a major one.

Just last year, I had a student who was the epitome of disorganization. He was not only failing my class, but several others as well. You know the type. Papers wadded up and crammed in books, no pen or pencil, lost his textbook, and so on. Even though I had checked with his guidance counselor and found out that money was not an issue with his family, I went ahead and bought him several inexpensive folders, I labeled them with all of his subjects, and I gave them to him along with a pack of pencils. I then offered to meet with him every day during his study hall to go over the homework assignments from each of his classes to help him stay organized (and hopefully pass). When I left school that day, I really felt good that I had come up with a concrete plan to help this student get back on track. The following morning, he returned my folders and my pencils and informed me that he didn't need my help.

As I've previously mentioned, some students, at least at this point in their lives, are either beyond—or they don't want—your help. Don't take it personally!

STUDENTS SLEEPING IN YOUR CLASSROOM

Although some of my peers might disagree, I refuse to condone this. As soon as someone's head makes contact with a desk, I'll walk right up to him and say, "[Name of student], are you okay? If you're sick, I'll write you a pass to go to the office, but if not, I can't let you sleep in here." I use a caring, concerned voice . . . unless it's a habitual offender. If so, I'll give him a detention and call his parents. That will often take care of it.

Some teachers disagree with the way I handle sleepers, claiming, "Hey, as long as he isn't disturbing me or the rest of my class, I let him sleep." It's a matter of personal preference, but I always think, "What would an administrator say if he walked into my class right now and saw a student sleeping?" I don't think any principal or assistant principal would condone such an action, and that's why I won't tolerate it.

INCESSANT TALKERS

I move talkers to the front of the room as soon as I identify them. If that doesn't do it, I tell the offender, "I've already moved you up front. The next step is out in the hall, and after that, it will be the office."

Another strategy I utilize is that I'll allow two students who are continually whispering to one another during class to continue doing so for the better part of a period, and then, only seconds before the bell rings (Timing is everything!) look at the two of them, point to a desk right up front, and state, "One of the two of you needs to move right up here as of tomorrow. I'll let you two decide which one will move." The next day, follow through with your plan and split up the talkers. Problem solved.

Don't worry about whether or not you are going to make anyone angry by moving him to the front. You'll make several decisions throughout the year that are going to make students angry . . . get used to it!

STUDENTS ASKING TO LEAVE YOUR ROOM

This is definitely a tough one. You certainly can't allow unrestricted use of your hall pass, but you definitely don't want to prohibit a student who is on the verge of vomit city or a teenage girl who has just started her menstrual cycle from leaving. I recommend the following approach: Make an announcement right at the end of class on the first day that students will not be permitted to leave your classroom unless in the case of an emergency. "Otherwise," instruct them, "don't even ask." I also add that if a student has to use the restroom, do so before class starts . . . just come in and let me know that you are headed to the restroom and that you may be a little late to class.

Then proceed to give them your interpretation of "emergency," especially since yours probably differs from that of a teen. What normally occurs as the school year unfolds is that because you went to the trouble of mentioning "only in case of emergency," the borderline-pee people won't even ask. However, if a student does ask, you should probably let him go.

Kids will also request to go places other than just the restroom. At our school, students request phone passes (used for going to the office to use the phone to call home). However, the number one reason that students will usually ask to leave class is to go to their locker. As far as this is concerned, understand that kids occasionally will forget their books or supplies. I usually let it go with just a warning . . . but if it becomes habitual, simply announce to the class that the warnings are over and that from this point on, detentions will be assigned if they come unprepared for class.

For those who always want to go somewhere at the end of class, just use the two-letter word "No." Don't ever forget that your students are your responsibility . . . keep them in your room as much as possible.

VULGAR LANGUAGE

This is one that requires some thought. Obviously you will not tolerate anyone shouting out an obscenity in your class, but what if during the final minute or two of the period your students are talking, and you hear someone—but you're not sure who—utter a "hell" or a "damn"? My advice is to simply say in a stern voice to everyone, "Hey, watch your language!" Don't go on a witch hunt trying to nail the culprit. Let's face it: The fact is that many of today's teens (and their parents) use these words in everyday conversation.

I never, however, let the word "shit" or the F-bomb go unpunished. This always warrants either an automatic detention or a trip to see the assistant principal. Use your own judgment, but be consistent.

How about in the hallways? As you walk through the halls during the changing of classes, you're likely to hear a lot of language unsuitable for younger audiences. Again my advice is this: A simple "Watch your language, please," is usually enough to gain the offender's attention. However, if you feel really strongly about it, and you happen to hear a student drop an F-bomb within earshot, you certainly have the right to assign him a detention or handle it according to your school's discipline code.

TWELVE

Another Effective Discipline Technique

Keep in mind that your job is to never allow a confrontation to erupt into a full-blown situation. Here's yet another valuable piece of advice: Although many discipline problems need to be resolved or handled on an immediate basis because timing is often very important, in some circumstances it's best to postpone resolving a potential situation.

For example, I have had many students during my twenty-one years in education question a grade on a paper or essay. English is obviously very subjective, and many times students—especially the high achievers—will question even a B on an assignment. Therefore, I've learned that when I return graded papers, I normally don't do so until the *end* of class. Then, as I hand them back, I always tell my students that if they are not happy with their grade or if they don't understand any of the comments that I have written, I will gladly meet with them after school or during common time, which is a thirty-minute period right after lunch where students can seek individual assistance from any teacher in the school.

The first thing this accomplishes is that it allows angry or unhappy students a chance to blow off steam before they come to see me. Whether it's in the hall on the way to their next class or at lunch, it's therapeutic for many students to criticize teachers with their friends . . . although most will commiserate, a few might look at the grade and honestly tell them that it was warranted. This also gives kids a cooling-off period where often the student will objectively analyze his paper in a realistic and unemotional manner. Lastly, it gives you a chance to listen and observe who isn't happy, and then you can prepare adequately for

69

those who come to see you. I've had times where I've misread a line or misinterpreted an idea in a paper and subsequently I've raised a grade because I made an honest mistake. However, when you put a potential confrontation off until later, what often occurs is that the student will never even come to see you.

I've also employed this strategy when it comes to discipline. I can vividly remember a confrontation with three students concerning a classmate they felt I had mistreated when I singled her out in class for not paying attention. These three paraded up to my desk at the end of class and began to discuss my treatment of this particular student. I had two options here. First, I could tell them that this was none of their business (which I wanted to do) and that if she felt she was being singled out it was *her* responsibility to talk to me. However, I instead told them that this really wasn't the right time, but that I'd be happy to meet with them tomorrow after school. Perhaps you can guess what happened. By giving them a full day to cool off, they not only didn't show up after school, I never heard another word about the supposed problem.

THIRTEEN

Stay Sharp! One of the Most Difficult Times to Maintain Order Is Right before Spring Break

This cannot be overstated. Depending on the part of the country where you teach, as the weather begins to change following the cold winter months of December, January, and February, the students, teachers, and administrators are ready for a break. And as spring break approaches, concentration wanes . . . and often student behavior reaches a yearly low. This is the time, even though it's near the end of your first year and you're probably feeling fairly confident of your teaching abilities by now, that you really need to be on guard.

After twenty-one years of teaching, you'd think that I'd be prepared for just about anything that could happen during the week right before spring break. But the following is yet another instance where I futilely attempted to keep a confrontation from becoming a situation.

It was on a Thursday, only two days before the start of our break, when an office worker came into the library (where we hold study halls) and informed me that one of my students was needed in the office. I was in charge of the study hall, so I immediately called out, "Lindsay, you're wanted in the office." She was seated in the back of the library, and without hesitation, she yelled back, "I just came back from there! I'm not going again!"

I was stunned. I knew that she was a new student who had been in our school only three weeks, and I also knew that some teachers were already complaining that she was cutting classes. But I hadn't encoun-

71

tered any type of problem with her, and I definitely wasn't ready for this reaction. I should have known better and remained calm, but when any student talks to me in a disrespectful tone, I sometimes forget my rule of pausing briefly to think before I speak. And this was one of those times. "Hey, don't shoot the messenger!" I yelled back at her, which would have been the end of my involvement if I had just stopped there. However, I chose instead to add, "And you need to lose that attitude." I turned to the office worker and told him to relay the message to the principal that Lindsay refused to go to the office. I really didn't know what would happen next, but it was out of my hands . . . or so I thought.

Minutes later, the principal arrived and took Lindsay out into the hallway, motioning for me to accompany the two of them. "What's going on?" he asked. Not waiting for Lindsay to respond, I told him that she was being disrespectful to me and that she refused to go to the office. "Okay. Thanks, Mr. Kitchen," he responded, and Lindsay was led away.

I hoped this was the end of it. After all, the period was nearly over, and spring break was only two days away. However, only a few minutes passed, and suddenly Lindsay was back—but she did not return to her seat. Instead, she went two tables over and plunked down next to a friend and began conversing. (Keep in mind that there were fifty-five students crammed into the library, and our school has a "No talking" policy in all study halls.) I didn't know what had transpired in the office, but there was no way I was going to allow Lindsay and her disrespectful attitude to get away with anything. However, instead of losing my composure, being the supposedly veteran teacher that I was, I calmly asked her to return to her seat. I was not going to let this malcontent get the best of me. Then it happened.

As she got up to return to her seat, she once again *yelled*, but this time to her friend, "Bye! I'll see you later!" Everyone looked, first at her, and then at me. I had two choices, and the first one in this case would have been the wiser of the two. I could either let this remark go, realizing that this girl was having a really bad day and that whatever happened to her in the office was just spilling over into my study hall, or I could act. I chose to act.

I did what I thought was the prudent thing at the time, which was instead of losing my temper, I went directly to the office and calmly asked our principal if he could remove Lindsay from my study hall—at least for this one day. He could see how upset I was, so he followed me back to the library and went right up to Lindsay and said, "Let's go." As she was leaving, she looked directly at me and said to the principal—and loud enough for the entire study hall to hear—"I'm going to hurt that man!" Students don't threaten teachers very often, but if it does ever happen to you, get your building administrators involved immediately! (Lindsay was suspended for ten days.)

In hindsight, if I hadn't said "And you need to lose that attitude," none of this probably would have happened. I allowed what should have been a relatively harmless matter to become a full-blown situation, and I should have known better, especially that close to spring break.

Just be alert and ready, and as trite as it might sound, "Expect the unexpected." In class, keep your students as busy as possible during every day of that final week before spring break, and in between classes, stand by your door. As I mentioned earlier in the book, you can prevent a lot of potential situations just by being visible.

FOURTEEN

What's the Best Way to Teach Your Subject?

REPETITION IS THE KEY TO SUCCESS

Certainly during your student teaching days you had the opportunity to experiment with various teaching techniques. You also should have learned a great deal by observing your supervising teacher as well as perhaps other staff members in your building. So I hope you have some ideas on how you plan to teach your subject long before your first day. However, I would like to share what has worked best for me and why it's been successful.

First, most of you are already aware that your students will normally fall under three categories of learning styles—visual, auditory, or kinesthetic—and that certain classes allow students more hands-on opportunities than others. You'll most likely use a combination of all three, but no matter what you do, *repetition* will be one of the most important keys to your success.

For example, I'm sure that you have been in a class (whether it is high school or college) where you were first assigned to read a collection of chapters (a "unit"), you then took notes while the teacher lectured on the material, and finally, you were tested on it. Next, you moved on to the following unit, and the process was repeated. At the semester break, you had an exam over everything you had supposedly "learned" throughout the first twenty or so weeks. Is this an effective method of teaching? It could be, but only if the teacher used each section to build off the previous one and continually reinforced the connections and correlation to previous units. The majority of the kids you teach will seldom recognize these connections, unless, that is, they are mentioned repeatedly.

I understand that all teachers have a specific curriculum guide to follow and that their students are accountable for all the material when they move up to the next level or grade. However, when information is covered only once, and then a student doesn't see it or hear it repeatedly leading up to the exam, how much of that material can an individual possibly retain? Although some students (and they're in the minority) are extremely bright and can grasp virtually any new concept or information the first time around, the majority of us don't learn that way! I'm not talking about memorizing information and then regurgitating it back on a test . . . just about anyone can do that! I'm talking about long-term memory, where a student retains information for years and possibly a lifetime.

I was a top-notch student in high school, but not because I was the smartest in my class; I was just really good at memorizing information. Unfortunately, when I got to college, I realized that in high school I had *learned* very little.

My theory is this: Repetition and reinforcing connections are the keys to learning! The majority of the material that I cover in my class is reviewed numerous times to the point where most students don't have any choice *but* to learn it. I teach my class the same way coaches coach their teams, the same way music and voice instructors teach their students, the same way that parents teach their kids to survive in society—repetition! If you played a sport or a musical instrument when you were younger, how did you prepare for competitions? You practiced! And you practiced the same skills, the same notes, the same plays, over and over and over until you learned them; in fact, you overlearned them. I teach the same way.

Please understand that I'm certainly not advocating that you say the same thing the same way each time. Although this method could be successful, kids nowadays would lose focus and eventually tune you out. Here's an example of how I employ the repetition method in my English class: I'm a firm believer in the importance of teaching vocabulary. I give my honors freshmen students twenty-five new words every Monday; first, I'll have them record the correct spelling of the word on the front side of a 3″×5″ card and the definition (which I provide) on the back. I also let them know the context in which the word is normally used. The students then have two days to memorize these definitions; on Wednesdays, I give an oral quiz where each student receives one word that he has to define aloud in front of the entire class. If he answers correctly, I record a 5/5 on my computer. On the other hand, if he misses the word, I record a zero, and the next person in the row then gets that same word.

The real learning occurs, however, in the preparation for the Friday tests. These evaluations are cumulative and cover every word that we've had since the first Monday of school. For example, on the final Friday of this past school year, my students were responsible for retaining the definitions of over 500 words . . . and they only received three of those words orally on the test. Because they are tested each week on every single word we've had the entire year, the students are forced to repeatedly go over past words as well as each week's new words. By the end of the year, although a student might not retain all 500 words, he certainly has learned in excess of 250 (at the minimum) . . . and because he has studied them so many times, they begin to appear almost routinely in his writing as well as in his speaking. Parents and students are amazed at how their vocabularies increase, and it definitely is not because of anything unique that I've done. When you practice the same skill (or word) enough times, it becomes learned behavior.

Let me cite another example of why reading, lecturing, testing, then moving on to the next section of chapters and repeating the process often doesn't work. In our school system, students are exposed to the eight parts of speech initially in the second grade. They also discuss and are tested on them in each successive grade. However, even knowing that students have been taught the material for the past six or seven years, I like to start each new school year by asking my freshmen to list and define the eight parts of speech. No class has ever averaged above 40 percent on this test, and it's obvious why: In the younger grades, the material is introduced, the students usually do some practice exercises out of a textbook, they are tested, and then they move on to something else. Most kids can't and won't learn this way! I cover the eight parts of speech during the first week of school, and then they continue to show up on quizzes throughout the entire year. They can't help but learn them . . . forever!

Thus, despite the stringent demands of your curriculum, continue going back over what you think is important *all year*! Constantly review! Don't allow kids to forget! It might often sound and feel like you're being redundant, but it works.

FIFTEEN

What You Can Expect from Your Principal and Assistant Principal

Hopefully you'll select a district with an experienced principal who will support you as well as consistently offer words of encouragement that first year. You'll probably deal more with the assistant principal, however, than the principal. Despite what you might have heard, the good administrators (both principals and assistants) want to help you with any problems whatsoever, in or out of the classroom. And the good ones will back you. Whether it's dealing with a student or a parent, 99.9 percent of the time a quality administrator sides with his teachers. Even if a teacher like you (or me) makes a mistake, good administrators let you know about it in private, but never in front of parents or students.

When I first started teaching, other faculty members in my building told me that if I couldn't handle my own discipline problems, I wouldn't be around very long. To a certain extent, this is true. Although I don't hesitate to send a student in the hallway, I seldom send students to the office. My advice to you is this: If ever a student issues a threat or shows blatant disrespect toward you (profanity or talking back), send the offender to the office immediately. Otherwise, if it's something less severe, either issue the student a detention or just have him stand in the hall for the remainder of your class period.

If you find yourself in a district—and there are several—that will not severely discipline those students who talk back or treat you with blatant disrespect, survive one year and then get out of there! I said this earlier, but it is certainly worth repeating: All schools and all districts are not

79

the same! In some schools, discipline is literally out of control, and this
happens mainly because administrators are not doing their job, which
ends up making a teacher's job miserable. Don't let this happen to you!
At the end of the school year, begin your search for another teaching
position. Don't give up! If you really enjoy teaching kids, you need you
to try again in another district.

Perhaps the most crucial dealings you'll have that first year with your
building principal will be during your observations. In most schools, all
new teachers are observed and evaluated at least twice by an administrator, and if you are part of a mentoring program you will also be observed by a member of your state licensure board. (In Ohio, it's called
"Praxis.") It can be a very stressful situation, but again, preparing and
overpreparing will minimize your anxiety. Then, when it's over and your
administrator reviews your evaluation, don't be afraid to ask questions.
And don't get defensive! This is an extremely difficult aspect of being a
principal, so any criticisms or recommendations offered are only meant
to help you. Even if you disagree with the comments or suggestions,
don't verbalize them. Immediately after you leave the office, take your
copy of the evaluation back to your room and read it over again, slowly.
If your administrator was critical in any way, formulate a plan that will
include any changes you are going to make.

If you don't agree with some of the comments, you can do one of two
things:

(1) Heed the advice, and make any adjustments per his recommendations, or (2) Ask a fellow staff member to come in one period to observe
you. After this occurs, ask for an honest evaluation of your performance.
If the teacher's opinion conflicts with that of your administrator, invite
him back to your classroom for a follow-up visit "off the record." Perhaps one of you just had a bad day.

SIXTEEN

What You Can Expect from Other Teachers

Depending on the district, don't expect all members of your new faculty to welcome you with the proverbial open arms. If you are coaching or if you have an interest in sports, you'll have the inside track to befriending many of the sports-minded faculty members, especially since the topic of athletics often dominates the lunch table conversation.

However, you must understand that young teachers attract a lot of attention from the students, and many older teachers could automatically resent you before they have a chance to get to know you. Still other colleagues might even view you as potential dating material.

A teaching staff is a small microcosm of society, with a slight lean toward the soap opera side. A large district could have many teachers who are either undergoing a divorce, dealing with a personal tragedy or illness, enduring hardships with their own children, and so on. In a smaller school, most perceive the faculty as more of a close-knit family type of group where everyone is willing to listen and be sympathetic, and for the most part, it's true. Thus, you might find yourself at the copy machine innocently preparing for your next period class when suddenly you are listening to a fellow faculty member who has a parent suffering from Alzheimer's disease. At times it can be depressing, but it's also a good feeling to know that someone feels comfortable confiding in you, and many teachers will do so simply because you're a new face.

The best advice I can give you is the same any parent would offer: Be nice to everyone, and don't take it personally if someone doesn't appear all too thrilled to have you on the staff. If you go into a district without knowing anyone, expect the situation to resemble that of a student attending a new school. Some groups (or maybe I should say "cliques") will attempt to befriend you and encourage you to join them, while others will have very little to do with you.

If you're not sure, try to mingle with as many different groups as possible, especially at lunch. During the first week or two, take turns going to the various places that staff members congregate to eat lunch or to relax, and then simply sit and listen. Ignore any negative comments some might have told you about other faculty members . . . judge for yourself. Be observant, listen more/talk less, and allow plenty of time that first year to find your niche on the faculty.

Some districts will place you on a team with three or four other teachers. This allows you to work closely with some of your peers and hopefully foster relationships that enable you, at times, to support one another. You get to share teaching and discipline strategies that might work with certain students who are posing problems for you or other teachers on the team. In most cases, this is a very healthy experience, especially for first-year teachers, because it offers that built-in support system you desperately need. Perhaps the only downside is if the members of your team don't work well together. If this occurs, don't get caught choosing sides against fellow team members. Don't ever forget that one of your many goals that first year is to *get along with everyone*.

Seventeen

The Types of Kids You'll Be Teaching

During your first year, you probably will be assigned the classes that no one else wants, so don't be surprised if it takes a while before you get to teach an honors class. Perhaps that won't matter to you, but the honors classes are the easiest to teach if for no other reason than discipline problems are usually minimal.

Aside from the honors classes, with inclusion you could be teaching students with a wide variety of ability levels. However, whether it's the students termed "gifted" or those who have severe learning disabilities, you must attempt to find the best way to teach everyone. If your school has the resources and finances, you might even have a special education teacher in a particular class or two to assist with those kids who have special needs.

More and more students nowadays are under the auspices of a 504 Plan or IEP (Individualized Educational Program) than ever before. These federally mandated programs outline services appropriate to students with documented disabilities.

Along with the special education teacher, the guidance counselor(s), the principal or the assistant principal, other classroom teachers, the parents, and sometimes legal counsel, you will be expected to attend meetings and then assist in organizing and documenting a plan to enable that student to be successful in the classroom.

When I was in school, a student who didn't pay attention was labeled as a troublemaker and someone who lacked self-discipline. That same student today is often diagnosed with a medical condition termed ADD (attention deficit disorder) or ADHD (attention deficit hyperactivity

disorder), and could have an IEP or 504, depending on how the disorder affects the student's school performance. As an educator, you must
be aware of all provisions and accommodations for the student in your
classroom. Failure to do this means you are not in compliance with the
law and could result in legal action against the district.

Examples of accommodations include extra time on tests, extended
deadlines for long-term assignments, an extra set of textbooks to keep
at home, extra study guides or chapter outlines to assist in preparing for
tests, etc. Some students are entitled to have special educators read test
questions aloud to them, and still others are afforded the opportunity
to listen to books on tape or on computer as opposed to reading them
silently.

As difficult as it might appear to sometimes remember and meet the
special needs of these students, constantly remind yourself that even
though it often creates extra work for you, it's not the child's fault that
he or she has the disability. Sure, some kids (and parents) will use this
as an enabling device and attempt to escape all responsibility for their
actions because of their "disability." On the other hand, however, many
of your LD students will never request nor expect any special attention
and will be the hardest workers in your class.

The meetings and special provisions that accompany 504 and IEP
students can be somewhat overwhelming, especially if they come the
day before school starts when you're trying to complete last-minute
tasks. But if you adopt the following philosophy, you'll always keep it in
proper perspective: If the student with the 504 or IEP were your child,
wouldn't you want (and expect) his teachers to do everything in their
power to help him succeed?

EIGHTEEN

Open House (Back-to-School Night)

Early in the school year, you will have what is referred to as "Open House" or "Back-to-School Night," where parents will come to meet you and hear about your class. It's a nerve-wracking event for me, even after twenty-one years, mainly because I obviously want to make a good impression with the parents of my students. And other than parent-teacher conferences, it's your only chance! Perhaps the main reason that I advocated sending a letter home to the parents on your very first day is so that they feel like they know you when they attend this function. Hopefully they'll enter with a positive attitude about you (thanks to the letter), and they'll leave feeling confident that their child is in good hands.

The key to success on this night, just like on your first day, is being prepared. Always give handouts! Most parents will enjoy listening to you, but they'll appreciate even more leaving with something they can take home and read at their leisure. I give every parent in attendance a copy of each of the handouts I've distributed to the students, and it seems to get a little longer each year. This past year, it was twenty-eight pages, which included a brief overview of the course, vocabulary and spelling lists for the entire year, the rules of commas, a proofreading checklist, etc. Sure, it took me a long time to put this together and copy, and I'm not advocating that you need a document anywhere near this lengthy, but you definitely need to give each parent *something* to take home.

At our school, the parents follow their child's schedule and spend eight to ten minutes in each class. If it's done in a similar manner in

85

your district, you probably won't have time to cover everything on your handouts, but it's better to have too much information than not enough. If you finish early, you could be setting yourself up for potential embarrassment or conflict. It's simply too easy for someone to put you on the spot by asking you a challenging question in front of a huge crowd of very important people, and some parents take tremendous pride in making new teachers squirm.

If someone insists on asking a question, unless it's an easy one, politely inform the parent that you'd be happy to speak with him or her immediately after the session is over. Don't ever allow anyone to force you into answering something you're not prepared for or don't want to handle . . . talk after class! If you have plenty of information on the handouts you distribute, *you* should be the only one talking the entire session.

NINETEEN

Parent-Teacher Conferences

Although many of my colleagues disagree, I consider this one of the most enjoyable times of the year, and it can be for you as well. Just like the rest of your teaching responsibilities, the key here is to be prepared. Many schools have conferences only once, and they're usually held two or three weeks into the second grading period. This gives parents a chance not only to review their child's first-term grade, but also to monitor the student's progress throughout the early stages of the second quarter.

Conferences are normally held over a two- or three-day period, and in many districts, parents will either sign up or call to reserve a time. What I like the most about conferences is that not only do I enjoy talking with the parents, I also gain valuable insight into a child's background, which often explains his performance and behavior (good or bad).

Don't ever go into a conference with the intention of just "winging it." I always begin by handing the parents a current grade-sheet printout, and this gives me a reference point for most of my comments. As soon as I finish covering the student's grades, I then discuss his behavior—good or bad. I'll end by asking if they have any questions, and I always answer them openly and honestly. If parents question whether or not their child is working up to his or her potential, I don't hesitate to tell them exactly what I see. If a student is not coming prepared for class or is not participating, again, I seize this opportunity to let the parents know. Most—if not all—parents will appreciate your honesty.

You'll usually find that the parents of those kids who are struggling in

87

your class are not the ones who will sign up for conferences. Instead, you'll end up meeting with the ones whose kids are excelling. However, always remember that parents never grow tired of hearing positive comments about their children. Many times I've said the following: "The two of you have obviously done a lot of really good things in raising her. I can only hope my daughter grows up to be just like her."

I've been through hundreds of conferences, and I can't recall a single one that didn't end on a positive note. I attribute this to the fact that parents appreciate the introductory letter that I send home at the beginning of the year, they enjoy all of the handouts I distribute at Back-to-School Night, and they respect the fact that I'm organized at the conference as well as honest.

If you would ever have to *initiate* a conference with parents because a student is misbehaving or underachieving, again, just be organized, prepared, and honest. Even if you must deliver the type of news they don't really want to hear, be candid, but then always try to end positively. I've often participated in meetings that involved the student, the rest of his teachers, and his parents. I remember saying the following about a former student who was causing a great deal of trouble for two of his other teachers:

> Ron, you have a tremendous amount of ability . . . but you're wasting it. Your friends might think you're funny now, but where are they going to be in five years? And where do you think you're going to be? You're immature, and if you don't stop and realize that you are making a fool of yourself on a daily basis, you won't be laughing when you start applying to colleges. Your parents are here because they care. Now, you need to start holding up your end of the bargain.

Inevitably, parents will thank me for being honest when they leave, whether I'm letting them know what an outstanding job their child is doing in my class or that he's constantly causing problems. And here's a valuable piece of advice I can offer you on how to handle parents as they *leave* your conference. On most occasions, parents will say, "If his grade begins to slip or he fails to do his homework, please call us." It's a legitimate offer, but what parents fail to realize is that you might have anywhere from 120–180 total students, and if you agreed to call every parent who asked you to each time his child's grade started to slip, you'd be spending way too much time on the phone. If a parent makes a similar request of you, don't just nod your head and say, "I will." Put the responsibility on the student! Instead, tell the parent, "It would be much easier if [name of student] asked me for a printout of his grades every Friday or gave me a sheet that I will gladly fill out on a weekly basis to keep you updated. Or, if it would be easier for you, please feel free to call me on a weekly basis. Just leave a message on my voice mail, and I'll get back to you as soon as I can." This way, the responsibility now rests with the student and/or the parent.

Behavior issues are handled differently. If a parent wants you to keep him updated on his child's behavior, tell him, "Don't worry . . . I'll definitely call you next week if you like and give you a progress report, or, I can simply call you if the situation doesn't improve." Then, simply abide by whatever the parent wishes.

One last word of caution: During a conference, if parents ever become confrontational with you, and on occasion some male parents will attempt to intimidate first-year teachers—especially females—just listen, be polite, and thank them for coming. Write down as much of what was said that you can remember, and then discuss it with your principal or assistant principal. On the other hand, if someone simply wants to argue and challenge everything you say, end the conference with the following: "I think it would be best if you called [name of principal] tomorrow and set up an appointment because I don't think we're going to agree on anything tonight." Then, as painful as it might be, thank the parent(s) for coming. Always be gracious! My mom's advice was extremely appropriate when she told me how to handle any disgruntled parent (she was a teacher for twenty-five years): "Kill 'em with kindness."

TWENTY

Handling Parent Phone Calls—Both Positive and Negative

Teachers need to contact parents at home or at work for many different reasons, but unfortunately, most call only to discuss negative situations (grades, behavior, etc.). I'll discuss calling home about grades later on in this chapter, but as far as behavior is concerned, I only call home (and I recommend you do the same) as a last resort.

For example, let's say your first two weeks have gone pretty smoothly. Sure, you've been challenged a few times, but you've passed each discipline and classroom management test up to this point. However, you have this one student in your third period class who just doesn't seem to get it. You've warned him repeatedly—you've even removed him from class once and given him a detention. You've talked with the rest of his teachers, with the assistant principal, and you've consulted his guidance counselor, but nothing is working. He is making the third period of your day a nightmare. This sounds like the appropriate time to call home and ask for parental help, right? You could, but first, consider this option: A veteran teacher once told me how to handle such a problem early in my career, and it's been an extremely successful strategy for me ever since.

During his first year of teaching, he had a student who was constantly talking, disrupting class, and being disrespectful. After repeatedly admonishing him in class during the first week of school, this teacher had had enough. He simply called the student out in the hall and asked him three basic questions:

91

1. "[Name of student], do you like me as a teacher? (Hopefully the student answers positively, but if not, you need to explore what type of problem he has with you. Then, continue.)
2. "Have I done anything to piss you off?" (Again, you hopefully already know the answer to this query, but by using the word "piss" he knows you're talking to him as an individual, mainly because that's a word many of your students use in everyday conversation. If he says "Yes," you obviously need to find out what you've done or at least what he *thinks* you've done and get it out into the open. However, if not, continue with one more question.)
3. "Then why are you causing so much trouble in my class and making it so hard for me to do my job?"

When the teacher utilized this strategy, not only did the student inform the him that he had no idea he was causing any trouble (he apparently acted that way in everyone's class), he apologized and was never a problem again. A simple two- to three-minute one-on-one conference and the matter was resolved. However, if this doesn't work, it's time to call home, inform the parents what's going on, and ask for their assistance.

Poor classroom performance is obviously another reason that teachers will contact parents. In our district, if a student is failing or even has a D at mid-term, we are required to call that student's parents. However, contrary to this type of call, which obviously is negative, I like to call three or four students' parents right after the grading period ends to give them *good* news.

For example, if a student has worked particularly hard to earn an A or B, I like to call home and let parents know how proud I am of the effort their child put forth throughout the quarter and how much of a pleasure it is to have him or her in class. Without question, these two or three phone calls you make after each of the first three grading periods are the most gratifying and appreciated calls you'll make all year.

Last year (at the end of the second grading period), I had a particular student who had worked extremely hard to raise his grade from an 89 percent (B) the first quarter to a 93 percent (A) the second. I called home and left a message (which, when leaving good news, is even better than directly talking to a parent because *everyone* in the family gets to listen, and the message can be saved and played repeatedly) regarding what an outstanding job the student had done and how hard he had worked to get his grade into the A range. I also mentioned what a quality person the student was and what a pleasure it was to have him in class. Again, because so few teachers choose to call home and mention anything positive, you'll have a family who will represent some of your biggest fans for as long as you remain in that district. Many of us in education sometimes forget that parents seldom get to hear the positives from teachers.

And I don't just choose to call the parents of the so-called "smart kids." Many of the lower-range ability students have *never* received any positive recognition for anything even remotely related to academics. Making a call to these homes will be something the family will never forget. I once called home just to remark what a privilege it was to have this particular student in my class and how proud I was of her for earning a C. On this occasion, I spoke with the girl's mother, and she started crying right on the phone. She then asked me if I would call her husband at work to relay the same message, and when I did, he was absolutely thrilled! It takes only minutes to make these types of calls, but the effects are often long lasting.

DEALING WITH THE NEGATIVE ONES . . . HOW TO DELIVER BAD NEWS

As far as the negative phone calls are concerned, my advice is simple: First, always be honest! Second, if you are returning a phone call, always do so within twenty-four hours. Third, if you are lucky enough to have a phone in your room that includes a voice-mail option, you'll obviously get to hear the recording and know why the parent called. However, if you simply get a message from the secretary to return a parent's phone call, you sometimes have no idea as to the nature of the call, but you still need to be prepared. Have all the grade information for that student directly in front of you as well as a few notes about behavior and effort so that you are as organized as possible.

Nearly all phone calls from parents are for three reasons:

1. They are questioning a grade (either on a particular assignment or the midterm/final grade for the quarter). It took me several years to get used to having parents call me to complain about or question a grade. In fact, I sometimes still get a little defensive, but then I remind myself that these parents are only standing up for their offspring, doing what they think is right, and that they are not always capable of being unbiased. When talking to any parent who is obviously upset over a grade (some might even cry), listen to the concern and then calmly explain yourself. Always remain calm! No matter what they say or how upset they might be, you need to maintain your composure.

2. Often parents are questioning an assignment, usually wanting to know more specifics. Even though you gave all the information necessary during class to complete the assignment and, in addition, distributed a handout explaining everything that you said, some students still don't understand. But instead of coming to you with questions, they take them home. Then, when parents don't know the answers, they might call you. Be patient with them . . . they only want what's best for their child.

3. Parents will almost *always* call if they think you are mistreating their child. Just keep in mind that when they call they almost never have the entire story—they're only getting their child's version. Once you explain what really happened, that parent will often thank you and the converstion will end. However, it's not always that easy. Just don't ever get into any type of argument with a parent over the phone. It's sort of like being an umpire . . . you are willing to listen—to a certain extent—especially because any discussion with a parent involving a child's wrongdoing can get very emotional. But if a parent continues to argue or debate, even after hearing your side, it's time to take it to a higher authority. That's what administrators are for. And if any parent ever issues a threat or verbally abuses you in any way, let your building principal know immediately! He will handle it!

   If the parent persists and begins to question or attack your credibility or integrity, politely say, "Mr./Mrs. [name], I'm really sorry that you feel that way. I would recommend that you call the office and set up a time when we can meet along with the principal."

Most parents don't want to take time out of their day to attend a meeting, especially in the principal's office, so always use this as your trump card to end an awkward conversation.

Let me give you a couple of examples of parent phone calls I've received and how I handled each. As I've mentioned throughout the book, I teach English, and along with my freshmen classes, I have two speech classes that are made up of juniors and seniors. On the very first day of school in my speech classes, I emphasize a rule that states that if a student is not prepared to give one of his four major speeches during the ten-week quarter, he will be dropped from the class immediately with an F and have to repeat the course (public speaking is a graduation requirement at our high school).

The following is what occurred: Scott was a member of my second period public speaking class, and he was (and always will be) the quintessential underachiever. He was lazy, unmotivated, and disorganized, but extremely intelligent. He was barely passing most of his classes because he simply didn't see the relevance of school and thus chose not to do the work. I held an individual conference with him on the very first day and reinforced the "Do not give speech, do not pass class" rule that I had just covered only minutes earlier with the entire class. He assured me that he understood the rule and its consequences, and he also informed me that he would be prepared for all of his speeches. And for the first one, he was.

However, on the date of his second speech (three weeks into the quarter), Scott asked for an extra day. No family emergency, no personal illness, no excuse . . . he simply wasn't prepared and wanted an extra day. Permission denied. I explained to him what was now going to happen, just like I had on the very first day, and although not pleased, Scott appeared to understand that he was going to have to accept the consequences of his actions. End of the story, right? No. Next, Scott's mom entered the picture.

When I arrived at school the following morning, the red light on my phone was flashing, indicating that I had at least one message. I knew it was one of Scott's parents who had called, and sure enough, it was his mom. I called her back immediately, and she wanted to know if it was true that her son had just failed public speaking, only three weeks into

the quarter. I calmly explained to her what the rule was, that it was discussed in detail on the first day of the quarter, and that everyone—
including Scott—was fully aware of the consequences. Her comment to
me was, "Do you really think it's fair to flunk a student without giving
him a second chance?"

Her question was a legitimate one; in fact, I probably would have
asked the same thing had it been my son. There will be phone conversations with parents during your first year and throughout your career
when you'll hang up and wish you had said something other than what
you did—I've done this countless times—but on this occasion, it worked
out perfectly. "Maybe you're right, ma'am," I began. "Maybe I should
give him a second chance. Even though I clearly explained to Scott on
the first day of class this rule and its consequences, and even though
when he asked if he could have an extra day and I told him that if he
didn't at least try to give his speech on that day he would fail for the
quarter and have to repeat the class—*even though I did all of these
things*—if you think the best thing for Scott is to let him off the hook
and give him a second chance, despite the fact that he was fully aware
of the consequences of his actions, I will abide by your wishes."

There was a brief pause, and then she spoke. "No, you're right," she
said. "He knew what was going to happen—he told me so. He'll just
have to take the class again next quarter."

Perfect! If only every phone conversation ended like that one, teachers could go to bed at night believing that all parents admire and respect
what we stand for. But for every parent like Scott's mom, there is another like Mr. Billings.

The problem with Mr. Billings was that he knew too much. (Sounds
like the beginning of a spy movie, doesn't it?) He was (and still is) an
English teacher at a neighboring school. In fact, he's the chairman of
his department. The controversy began a few days after I returned his
son's English paper in my honors class (the grade was $B-/C+$). Initially he called to "voice his concerns" (always be ready for battle when
a parent uses this subtle phrase). After twenty-one years in education,
I've come to realize that parents who aren't teachers simply call to complain, but teachers who are also parents call to "voice their concerns."

Mr. Billings's concern was that although I had commented negatively
on his son's performance regarding grammar and punctuation, I hadn't

focused nearly enough on the positives—especially regarding content. Had he sat in my class every day to hear the directions as well as the criteria that I was using on this particular assignment for evaluation purposes, Mr. Billings perhaps would have understood the reason for the grade. But maybe not. This was obviously the case of a very proud English department chairman who was angry and offended over the fact that, in his opinion, his son had been unfairly criticized for below-average punctuation and grammar skills. He even went so far as to pass the paper around to his colleagues in the English department, and they all concurred with their chairman (big surprise, right?).

After several voice-mail messages left by each of us, we finally spoke, and during our conversation, I listened to his concerns and then calmly explained the criteria that I used for this particular paper weighed heavily on grammar and punctuation. However, he still disagreed with the grade I had given his son and continued to reiterate his point about why I should have focused more on the content of the paper. Once I realized that nothing was going to be resolved, I suggested he call the principal and set up a meeting. (Again, don't ever argue with a parent!) This was one of the few times in my career that the parent actually followed through and set up a meeting with our building principal.

Ultimately, the principal listened to his side, then reiterated my position (I just sat and listened), and the meeting ended. We basically agreed to disagree. Thus, when in doubt, stand your ground, but don't argue—politely tell the parent to call the principal and set up a meeting.

TWENTY-ONE

Professional Development (In-Service Days and Educational Seminars/Workshops)

Unfortunately, although you might occasionally experience a seminar or workshop that is worthwhile and applicable to your teaching, these days are often a complete waste of time. In fact, don't be surprised if you find yourself bored and even angry over the fact that someone who seems to know very little about teaching is wasting your day—and making a lot of money doing so. You'll end up viewing in-service days the same way many teachers do: It's the next best thing to a holiday because you don't have any students.

In most districts, attending seminars and workshops is encouraged. Nearly all administraors love the term "continuing education" for their teachers, and most gladly pay for a day away from school if they believe it will improve an educator's job performance. Although some teachers enjoy attending, I despise them for several reasons. The first problem is that even though the literature previewing the seminar usually sounds impressive, the presenter often falls far short of making it interesting or applicable to my classroom. In addition, all too often I find myself using a plethora of elementary school supplies (crayons, paste, construction paper, stickers, etc.) to create role-playing activities that are a complete waste of time to most high school educators. However, what I've found to be one of the biggest deterrents—at least in my own situation—is that when I miss a day of school, I ultimately spend more time preparing for a substitute teacher than I would have spent preparing and teaching the lesson myself . . . and I don't like leaving my students in someone else's hands.

Although I view in-service days as a nice break from students, I avoid most seminars and workshops because I don't feel comfortable relinquishing my classroom to a relative stranger. (You'll completely understand what I mean once you've spent some time in your classroom teaching your students.) If you find something that interests you and your district will pay for it, go at least once, and then make your own decision if it was worthwhile.

TWENTY-TWO

Peaks and Valleys . . . Enjoying the Good Days while Surviving the Bad Ones

If you heed my advice (when appropriate), you will have many more good days than bad ones during your first year. When you leave school after a good day, you'll feel almost invincible, like there is no hurdle too difficult to overcome. These times are obviously easy to handle, but as far as the bad ones are concerned, that's what family and friends are for.

Expect some bad days! When you're dealing with people, especially teenagers, your days from 8:00 a.m. to 3:00 p.m. will be totally unpredictable. And during those difficult times when you seriously begin to question why you ever wanted to get into education (and during that first year, you'll have some of these), you must continually remind yourself that the next day will be better . . . and it usually is.

But what if the bad days outnumber the good ones? During those first few weeks and months, this could very well happen. In most cases, this is normal! Remember, no matter how prepared you are, you will still make some mistakes, but as long as you learn from them, by Thanksgiving (and probably sooner) you should feel like you are in some sort of teaching groove. If, however, by Thanksgiving you feel mired in a hopeless situation, and a good day never seems to follow a bad one, do this: Give someone a chance to help you! Meet with your building principal or guidance counselor and discuss your feelings. Don't continue to allow yourself to be miserable without seeking advice or assistance; it's not fair to you and it's not fair to your students.

Then, if the situation hasn't improved by Christmas, alleviate the pressure by acknowledging to yourself (*but not to anyone else at school*) that this will be your first and last year in that particular district. But before making your final decision, talk about your feelings with at least one teacher you have befriended throughout the year as well as with your family. Solicit opinions as to whether they feel your negative experience should be attributed to that particular school or the profession in general. As I've mentioned several times, not every school is the same, but perhaps even more importantly, some who enter the profession just weren't meant to be teachers.

I highly recommend keeping a file of all the positive feedback you get from your students, parents, or administrators. Even now, I still have a few bad days, but I find comfort—thanks to all my years of experience—knowing that the next day will be better, and it always is. I also occasionally read through a few of the many positive notes I've received over the years, and instantly I gain comfort and reassurance.

Let me give you one example of what was a disastrous day for me during my first year, but how it later turned out to be something really positive. As I mentioned earlier, I had cafeteria duty that first year. However, I really didn't mind. I viewed it as an opportunity not only to chat with the kids I taught and coached, but also to get to know many students that I didn't teach. One of the biggest problems with any cafeteria—except, of course, for the kids complaining incessantly about the food—is waiting in line. Teenagers are notoriously impatient people. Therefore, when the lunch bell would ring, dozens of students—sometimes in a full sprint—would come from all directions to beat the rush. One of my main responsibilities quickly became to stand guard where the line formed and make certain everyone slowed down to eliminate the possibility of trouble, whether that meant someone falling or someone cutting in line. Eventually, the trick for some students became to use the restroom during the final few minutes of the class they had right before lunch . . . and then simply get in line early. That's exactly what caused the potentially disastrous situation (and it was indeed a full-blown situation) I encountered.

Luke was one of the most feared juniors in the entire class. He would frequently be the topic of conversation on Monday mornings regarding which couples had broken up or who beat up whom. (If you remember from earlier in the book, I alluded to the fact that it wasn't uncommon for male students to arrive at school on Mondays with black eyes or bruised faces from weekend fights at the local drive-in.) Luke was often the name circulating as the victor—I never saw any trace of a bruise on him—and he often unbuttoned his shirt nearly to his waist to show off what most girls considered a "studly" chest.

On this particular day, as I was standing at the end of the hallway near the main entrance to the cafeteria awaiting the all-out charge to consume the very same food the students loved to complain about, I noticed Luke strolling toward me. When I asked him where he was supposed to be, he just smiled and said, "Come on, Mr. Kitchen. I just don't want to wait in line today . . . I'm really hungry." I immediately sent him back to class—at least I thought that's where he was heading. Approximately one minute after Luke disappeared from my sight, the bell rang, and guess who never went back to class and thus was the very first person in line? My man, Luke.

I approached him just as he reached for his tray and silverware—and just as dozens of students flocked to get in line behind him. "Luke," I began, "you didn't go back to class, did you?"

"Oh, come on now, Mr. Kitchen. I told you I was hungry." He began to slide his tray along and go past me, but I stood in front of him, foolishly blocking his path. (You would have thought I would have learned my lesson after my experience with Jake . . . remember the man-child? Never back a student into a corner!)

"Luke, you need to go to the end of the line," I informed him in a nonthreatening tone. After all, I thought this was only fair. He'd deliberately disobeyed me, but instead of overreacting and giving him a detention or making a big deal of it, I felt going last in line was an appropriate punishment. I gently grabbed his arm and attempted to guide him toward the rear of the line. What he said next totally stunned me . . . you see, I had Luke in my English class, and, up until this point, he'd always treated me with the utmost respect. But this time, Luke snapped.

"I'm not going anywhere with you. Take your fucking hands off me!" he yelled, as he jerked his arm away from my light grasp. Uh oh . . . another of those situations where I was caught totally off guard.

"Come on, Luke, let's go to the office" was the only thing I could think to say at that point. A huge crowd was now gathering as oncoming students flocked to the lunch line, and Luke wasn't budging.

"I said I'm not going anywhere with you!" he repeated, his voice still raised.

I realized this kid indeed wasn't going to acquiesce, so I calmly said to him, "Luke, you're making a big mistake." With that, I headed toward the office alone and reported the confrontation to our assistant principal. And as tough a character as Luke was, I think he knew he had screwed up, especially when the assistant principal told me he met Luke in the hall . . . walking in the direction of the office.

Luke was suspended, but the biggest shock of this entire ordeal came about a week after this incident. I received a letter from Luke (while he was on suspension) apologizing for what he had done and stating how much he liked and respected me. Wow! I remember leaving school that day feeling like I was truly making a difference, at least in one student's life.

Unless someone actually tells you, it's often difficult to ascertain exactly what, if any, impact you've had on your students. Teaching is like an assembly line, but you seldom get to view the finished product. I often wonder what's happened to some of the many students I've taught or coached over the years, but unless I run into them somewhere, I seldom learn the answer. Our profession can be very discouraging at times, but it only takes one Luke every now and then to let you know that you are indeed making a difference.

Twenty-Three

Helpful Hints

DON'T MAKE WAVES YOUR FIRST YEAR

When you join your new faculty, especially if the majority of staff members are veteran teachers and somewhat older, don't be overzealous in implementing new ideas (listen more, talk less).

Don't misunderstand . . . if you're asked, be tactful, and state your opinion. However, if it's not solicited, don't offer it—at least not until you've had time to gain the respect of your peers. Not all members of your new faculty will be ready to hear about all the innovative ideas you might have learned during your student teaching experience or most recent college classes. So unless you're asked, don't offer. You'll certainly have enough work tending to your own classroom without trying to "fix" the problems of your school or district. Therefore, when attending teachers' meetings, *listen* and *observe*, and speak only when spoken to. If you have questions, try to save them for after the meeting. Teachers' meetings are notoriously longer than they need to be, so whenever possible, ask your questions after the meeting

AVOID STEREOTYPING YOUR STUDENTS

Although teachers should never be judgmental, many of us are. In fact, it's a problem I struggled with in my early years, and I know many of my colleagues did as well. I attribute this to my upbringing; I was never exposed to the baggy style of clothing, the body piercings, or the "gothics," so the first thought I had when I saw this type of student was an extremely narrow-minded one: "This kid is a punk."

Early on in my teaching career, I'll never forget the day Jeremy came strolling into my class. Although he was a new student, he certainly knew how to make an entrance—and an immediate impression. His clothes were the type that I'd never allow my own children to wear. He had the baggy look . . . the waist part of his jeans was so low I'd swear that Jeremy was a plumber in a previous lifetime. He wore a black rock-and-roll T-shirt, he had long greasy hair, and he entered my classroom only minutes after I'd started my lesson and announced, "I'm here!" No doubt Jeremy had done this before.

I lost my composure. I immediately shot back, "Hey, when you come into this room you do so with your mouth shut, or I'll send you right back to wherever you came from. Is that understood?" He didn't respond, but as he walked slowly to an open seat in the front of the room, I feared the worst. He had that look of being nothing but trouble for the next eight and a half months. But I was wrong.

After that first day, Jeremy continued to dress in the same manner, but as the days and weeks passed, I got to know him as a person. After watching him interact with his peers and participate in classroom discussions, I discovered he was a warm, sensitive, and caring individual who was now in his fifth school in nine years (his father was in the military). In fact, he became one of my favorite students, and three years after rudely interrupting my class on his first day at our school, I did something I seldom do for any student—I attended his graduation party.

Every veteran teacher has had the experience of prejudging a student on the first day because of a certain look or style of dress, only to later discover this individual was compassionate, intelligent, and a pleasure to teach. But it will also work the opposite way. At some point, you'll look at a student who is neatly attired and appears to be polite and trustworthy, but he'll turn out to be one of the biggest jerks in your class.

Many kids choose to be different by dressing a certain way or wearing their hair in an alternative style. Give each of your students the same opportunities and get to know all of them before you start to judge anyone.

BE FAIR IN WHAT YOU ASSIGN . . . LISTEN
TO YOUR STUDENTS

This goes back to the power-trip theory. Listen to your students and be realistic about your expectations. You certainly don't want to be perceived as a pushover, but at the same time, if students have a major assignment due in your class on a particular Friday and the history teacher and the math teacher also have projects due on the same day, it's okay to extend your deadline. The message you are sending is that you are willing to listen to your students, and you have sympathy and compassion for them.

Too many teachers think that their class is the most important one, and they totally ignore the fact that their students have six or seven *other* classes. (Do you remember the type?) Don't be one of these teachers! Sure, deadlines are important, and I'm not suggesting you move yours back every time it conflicts with someone else's, but there is no harm in giving in if you're doing so for the right reasons.

Even though I feel that a very important part of my job as an educator is to teach my students how to budget their time and accept responsibility, I tell my students repeatedly that although my goal is to challenge them, I'm not out to make their lives miserable. I understand that kids are involved in more extracurricular activities nowadays than ever before, and I encourage—as do colleges—all students to be well-rounded and to get involved. As a first-year teacher, I'd recommend that if you *do* choose to extend a deadline for an entire class, let them know this is a one-time occurrence. Then, even if they ask again—and they probably will—you can simply say, "Sorry, I told you last time this would only happen once."

UNION VS. NONUNION: BE AWARE
OF THE PROS AND CONS

Many public schools belong to a teachers' union, which is the group that will protect your rights as an educator. However, even if your district as a whole does not belong, you'll still have the opportunity on an individual basis to join your teachers' association. It will be similar to but just

not as powerful as the union would be. Perhaps the only drawback is
the dues, which could range anywhere from approximately $400–$800,
but if the need arises, especially if you are ever sued, the union will
provide free legal support. Think of it as a $400–$800 insurance policy.
In my twenty-one years of education, I've luckily never had the need for
any type of legal support; however, nowadays you can never predict
what parents are likely to do when it comes to their children.

DON'T TEACH SUMMER SCHOOL

Use your summers to relax as far away from school as possible. You need
this time away from school to recover and refuel for next year. If you
need to earn extra income over the summer, work as a camp counselor
or manage a local swim club, two places that like to hire teachers. Do
not teach summer school!

BEHAVE APPROPRIATELY IN AND
OUT OF SCHOOL

When you're a new teacher—especially in high school—some of your
students might only be four or five years younger than you. It's an unavoidable fact that some of them will at times flirt with you. Be on
guard! If you have a student who is being extremely forward, let your
principal know immediately! Don't ruin your career over a hormonally
driven teenager.

Also, never drink alcohol on school grounds under any circumstances,
and avoid drinking excessively in any public place where there's even
the slightest chance you might see one of your students. You are a repre-
sentative of your school, and you are expected to set an example at all
times. If you can't abide by this concept, you're in the wrong profession!

BEGIN PURSUIT OF YOUR
MASTER'S DEGREE

It's best to begin work toward your master's degree as soon as possible,
but I recommend waiting until the summer following your first full year

of teaching for the two reasons: First, you want to be sure that you are in the right profession before you start paying for classes you might not need. After your first year, you should have a pretty good idea if teaching is really what you want to do. Second, during that first year, give your undivided attention to being the best teacher you can be. If you do your job correctly, you won't have time to take any graduate classes.

DRESS THE PART

During your first year, look professional at all times (no blue jeans). Even if your school allows casual dress, don't do it your first year; men should always wear a shirt and tie and women should either wear a dress or blouse/sweater and appropriate slacks.

Although some might claim that what you wear doesn't affect your ability to teach, it *does* affect how your students look at you and the professionalism you bring to the job. If you want to be respected and treated like a professional, dress the part! Unless it's an isolated event (for example, "Spirit Week," where a particular day of that week might be designated as "jeans day"), there are no exceptions to this rule for first-year teachers!

KEEP DETAILED LESSON PLANS

Most districts will require that you keep some type of lesson plans, and many administrators might even collect or at least check them on a weekly or monthly basis. During your first year, this will guarantee that you'll remain organized and focused on sticking to a plan. (Plus, you'll be able to use these as you plan your second year.) I've already mentioned about good teachers being flexible and how it's virtually impossible to predict how long it will take to effectively teach each aspect of your curriculum, especially that first year. However, perhaps the most important ingredient of lesson plans is that they will include an up-front explanation to your students as to the methods as well as the goals of the lesson (i.e., pupil performance objectives).

I feel strongly that kids need to be told honestly the rationale behind an assignment so that they can establish the connections that I referred to back in chapter 14. Then, as you gain more experience, you'll feel much more confident knowing how and when to present certain lessons without having to necessarily write everything down in a formal manner.

BE RECEPTIVE TO A MENTOR

As I mentioned in a previous chapter, you might be assigned a mentor (veteran teacher) who will guide you through your first year. In fact, I recently completed a class called *Pathwise*, which taught me how to be a mentor in accordance with Praxis, the current governing body of all new teachers in the state of Ohio (as well as several other states in the near future).

Although the purpose is sound, the process can be extremely intimidating to a new teacher. In addition to the many pressures you will be facing your first year, if you are under the auspices of Praxis, you also will be working with a mentor to prepare you for a state evaluation that you must pass in order to receive your license. Don't panic! Before your observation, you'll get at least a month to become acclimated to your new profession, and you get to prepare a lesson specifically for that day when you are evaluated. Most teachers succeed on the first attempt, but if something goes wrong on your first try, you will receive two additional opportunities to qualify for licensure.

I agree that first-year teachers can benefit from a mentor whom they can confide in and possibly work with on a daily basis, but I don't like the fact that you are forced to audition for someone outside of your district who has never previously set foot inside your classroom. In addition, as I mentioned earlier, as a new teacher, you have enough to worry about without additional concerns over this process. However, if you must endure a process such as Praxis just make sure you choose a lesson that you feel extremely comfortable with for your evaluation day, and then warn your students for days and possibly even weeks in advance about the importance of this event for you.

ESTABLISH A PLAN FOR MAKE-UP WORK

This is without question one of the biggest headaches for all teachers. In our district, we have a "Homework Hotline," where parents and students can call the school, access a teacher's voice mail, and hear the homework assignments on a daily basis. This has been very successful, but if you don't have such a system in place at your school, the following plan worked well for me (before we got the Homework Hotline): During the first week of school, I'd tell each student to find a homework partner, and I'd then collect the partner's name and phone number so I could keep this information in my records. If a student was absent from school, he would call his partner to learn what he had missed. If someone didn't feel comfortable with this option, he could obviously then talk to me. (Just make sure that you don't allow students to come to you at the beginning of class to find out what they've missed—this delays the start of your class and invites commotion and chaos. Make them wait until the end of the period!)

When a student returns from an absence, the normal policy is to allow him the same amount of days to make up work that he missed from school. (For example, if John misses two days of school, he gets two days to submit his make-up work, unless he talks to me and makes other arrangements.) The key is communication on the part of the *student* . . . make it the student's responsibility, not yours, to complete make-up work.

Then, when someone submits the work, either place it immediately into a designated folder until you get time to grade it, or grade it right away and record the score. If you don't place it in a special folder or grade the work immediately upon receiving it, you'll lose it. Stay organized!

UTILIZE YOUR PLANNING
PERIOD EFFECTIVELY

Every teacher has one planning period per day to write lesson plans, grade papers, return parent phone calls, make copies, or take care of personal business. Other than lunch, it will seem like the shortest period you have, especially because so many teachers waste it. As a first-year teacher, you must take advantage of this time! Don't read the paper, surf the Internet, or spend the period conversing with other teachers about last night's game. Organization is crucial during that first year, so at the very least, use this hour to prepare lesson plans, notes, or assignments for your upcoming classes. Don't waste time!

DON'T SWAMP YOURSELF . . .
HAVE A PERSONAL LIFE

A typical mistake made by first-year teachers is piling on the work for fear of being labeled "soft." First of all, stick to your original plan (syllabus) that you made up weeks in advance of your first day. Don't worry about what other teachers in your department might be assigning. Sure, you will always welcome advice from veteran teachers, but don't get caught up in worrying what everyone else is thinking . . . do what *you* think is right. But don't pile on the work! Kids have lives outside of school and so should you; don't spend your weekends grading papers. And even when you assign homework, don't feel like you always have to grade it. Sometimes I just walk up and down the rows to make sure everyone has the assignment, and then I'll immediately record a score of 10/10 or 0/10 for a homework grade.

As far as getting involved with your school, there's certainly nothing wrong with volunteering to help out with homecoming, assisting with a school dance, or attending the football game on Friday night, but don't make the mistake I made of spending every spare moment of your first year at school. I volunteered for every committee, helped out with every school dance, and coached three sports . . . this was a huge mistake! Teachers need time away from school to spend with family and friends. This will ensure that your love of teaching remains fresh and strong.

And finally, just so you are aware, any type of misconduct by students at a school function (sporting event, school dance, etc.) is still subject to penalty by the school. I'll never forget the time a student, whom I'd given a detention to earlier in the day, told me to "fuck off" at a football game. What he failed to realize was that saying this to me at a Friday night football game was the same thing as saying it to me in the hallway during school hours. The following Monday, I reported the incident and the student was suspended.

ACCEPT RESPONSIBILITY
FOR YOUR ACTIONS

Even though many in the business world would argue that teachers aren't entitled to a bigger salary because we only have to teach five or six classes in a day and we get summers off, very few jobs in business require an individual to be as prepared and focused on a daily basis as teaching does. The spotlight is on a teacher for anywhere from 250 to 300 minutes every day, and at times you will make mistakes. But don't worry . . . there will always be twenty-five to thirty critics in your classroom willing to point them out. In fact, some students revel in the opportunity to catch teacher errors. Here's how you handle this situation: Just laugh it off!

If you aren't sure, whether it's how to spell a word correctly or how to interpret a school policy, look it up or ask someone before you say it out loud or write it on the board. There's no excuse for being lazy!

I never have been nor will I ever be afraid to admit an honest mistake. If, for example, it involves a student's grade, I'll just apologize, correct the error, and move on. I've had situations where a simple data entry error has ultimately cost a student a higher final grade, and usually the student doesn't catch the mistake—I do. I could easily proceed, knowing that the error will go undetected, but instead, I'll make the correction. However, I would recommend using your best judgment if the error would end up *lowering* the student's grade . . . I normally don't make the change if I've already told the student and it involves dropping a grade by only one letter, unless there are extenuating circumstances. In cases like these, you have to do what feels right to you. Just remember this about grades: They'll mean a great deal more to your students and their parents than they ever will to you.

SAVE YOUR MONEY! BEGIN INVESTING
IMMEDIATELY IN A 403B

As of 2003, all teachers are allowed to defer up to $12,000 of their total income into a mutual fund—this account is called a "403b." The money is not taxed and will be deducted from your gross income. Even though you are not required to invest anything, this is an opportunity that no teacher should pass up! You decide how much you want to invest each pay period by filling out the proper paperwork. Then, the designated amount is deducted from each of your paychecks and forwarded to the mutual fund company of your choice. (I invest $250 per month, and I try to increase it by $50 per month every year.) All the money that you invest during your teaching career will continue to draw interest, and upon retiring, you should have a very healthy sum to supplement your retirement income.

As I mentioned earlier, soon after you're hired, visit the school treasurer and ask for the appropriate forms to *manage your own 403b*. Some districts require you to go through their representatives and invest only in specific funds, but most will allow you to manage your own . . . if you ask.

Unfortunately, I didn't begin investing until I had already been teaching for ten years, and I lost out on thousands of dollars of deferred income that could have been invested and earning interest during that entire period. Although there are no guarantees, wise investments could potentially earn you at or close to double-digit interest rates (over the long term), and upon retirement, you will have amassed quite a large sum of money to supplement your teacher's retirement. Start your 403b account immediately!

TWENTY-FOUR

Final Thoughts

There aren't many certainties when dealing with teenagers, but at some point during your year—whether it is during the first day or the first week—you will be tested. And it might not be attributed to anything you did or didn't do. Some kids simply can't help themselves. Many are coming to you from a world of abuse, neglect, addiction, apathy, or divorce. Others deal with serious social deficiencies or severe learning disabilities, and for these children every day is a struggle.

But when the bell sounds and your door closes, you are left to teach them, and at times to help hold their lives together. Although you might not successfully handle your first "test," or even your second or third the same way you would after you gaining some valuable experience, it's okay. Even now, after twenty-one years, I still make mistakes—we all do. However, I'm committed to the profession, and I love what I do. Whatever situation arises, if you act not out of anger or malice, but instead out of kindness and caring, you'll do the right thing most of the time, and ultimately you'll be well on your way to a successful career as an educator.

I hope you have learned something from my book and my experiences. We need good teachers who are willing to accept the responsibility of being a positive role model and help make a difference in the lives of today's teens . . . we need *you*.

INDEX

ABOUT THE AUTHOR

Robert Scott Kitchen has been involved in education for twenty-one years. After a three-year teaching stint fresh out of college, he temporarily retired to pursue a lifelong dream in professional baseball administration. However, missing the classroom, he returned to education in 1987, substitute taught for one year, and has spent the last sixteen years teaching English at a small suburban high school in Cincinnati, Ohio. His career in the classroom has been at the high school level, but he has coached kids in various sports from grades 4 through 12. Bob received his undergraduate degree from Miami University and his master's from Western Illinois University.